Rediscovering mixed-use streets

This publication can be provided in other formats,
such as large print, Braille and audio.
Please contact:
Communications, Joseph Rowntree Foundation,
The Homestead, 40 Water End, York YO30 6WP.
Tel: 01904 615905. Email: info@jrf.org.uk

Rediscovering mixed-use streets

The contribution of local high streets to sustainable communities

Peter Jones, Marion Roberts and Linda Morris

JOSEPH ROWNTREE
FOUNDATION

First published in Great Britain in 2007 by

The Policy Press
Fourth Floor, Beacon House
Queen's Road
Bristol BS8 1QU
UK

Tel no   +44 (0)117 331 4054
Fax no   +44 (0)117 331 4093
Email   tpp-info@bristol.ac.uk
www.policypress.org.uk

© University of Westminster 2007

Published for the Joseph Rowntree Foundation by The Policy Press

ISBN 978 1 86134 985 9

Transferred to Digital Print 2008

British Library Cataloguing in Publication Data
A catalogue record for this book is available from the British Library.

Library of Congress Cataloging-in-Publication Data
A catalog record for this book has been requested.

Peter Jones is Professor of Transport and Sustainable Development at University College London; he was previously Director of the Transport Studies Group at the University of Westminster. **Marion Roberts** is Professor of Urban Design at the University of Westminster. **Linda Morris** is a former research fellow, Transport Studies Group, University of Westminster.

The **Joseph Rowntree Foundation** has supported this project as part of its programme of research and innovative development projects, which it hopes will be of value to policy makers, practitioners and service users. The facts presented and views expressed in this report are, however, those of the authors and not necessarily those of the Foundation.

Cover photograph: Linda Morris
Cover design by Qube Design Associates, Bristol
Printed and bound by CPI Group (UK) Ltd, Croydon, CR0 4YY

Contents

List of tables and figures

Tables

Figures

Acknowledgements

This research originated from an idea first proposed by the Independent Transport Commission.

We would like to thank Alex Upton, Budhi Mulyawan and Pushpa Arabindoo for their invaluable research assistance with various parts of the study.

We would like to thank the Project Advisory Group for its assistance and support throughout the research. The group comprised Paul Anstee, Simon Barnett, Linda Beard, Terence Bendixson, Tom Bolton, Chris Glen, Michael Hebbert, Robert Huxford, Peter Matthew and Elizabeth Shove.

Many people provided valuable advice and assistance in each of the case study areas, in particular, in Coventry, the late Colin Eastman, Victoria Giffert, Steve Ancell, Barry Cox and Nick Richards; in Tooting, Audrey Helps, Norman Frost, Mark Wiltshire and the Tooting Partnership Board; and in Sheffield, David Whitfield, Colin Harvard, Nick Silvani and Ben Benest.

We were also assisted in parts of the research by Tim Grosvenor, Philip Connolly, Christine Binne and Che Sutherland.

Finally, we would like to thank JRF Project Manager, Katharine Knox, and her colleagues at JRF for their support, advice and assistance throughout the project.

All the photographs in this report were taken by members of the research team. The CCTV footage was provided by, or on behalf of, Coventry City Council and Wandsworth Borough Council.

Summary

The mixed-use street, or local urban high street outside a main city centre, is rising in importance on the government's policy agenda, as it has the potential to address several current policy concerns. In relation to sustainability, in environmental terms it enables people to shop locally without cars, in economic terms it provides a well-connected catchment area of customers for local businesses, and in terms of social sustainability it provides inclusive places for local communities to participate in different activities and to meet one another. In terms of the liveability agenda, the local high street can be a pleasant and stimulating place for people to travel through and to visit as a destination in itself.

Yet mixed-use streets have frequently suffered from neglect. There are various reasons for this, but the key issue lies in their dual function as 'links' in a movement system that connects places and as destinations, or 'places', in their own right. Prominence has traditionally been given to these streets' link role and to enabling traffic to move through the area quickly, in preference to enhancing their qualities as places for local residents, businesses, shoppers and visitors. The fragmentation of responsibility for looking after the street, on the part of agencies and professions, has also caused problems. Changes in retailing patterns, whereby shopping has been concentrated in large shopping precincts in town centres and in out-of-town developments, have weakened the traditional commercial base for local mixed-use high streets and starved their public spaces of significant investment.

The starting point of this study was a concern to better understand the significance of these streets to people, as spaces of connection through which they travel, as places to shop, meet and pursue other activities, and as spaces that contribute to local identity. The aim was to investigate and record all of the varied aspects of daily life on three case study streets – what people did there and what they felt about the streets. The study investigated sections of mixed-use local high streets in inner-suburban areas: Ball Hill in Coventry, London Road in Sheffield and the sections of street surrounding the Upper Tooting Road/Mitcham Road intersection at Tooting Broadway in South London. Each lies within a substantial residential catchment area that has suffered from some degree of social deprivation or enjoys a strong ethnic mix.

Particular attention was paid to the potential conflicts that could arise through the high street's dual function as both a link and a place. A wide variety of research methods was employed, including collating a broad range of existing data; carrying out traffic and pedestrian counts; using CCTV footage to observe behaviour; and using questionnaires to carry out household, business and on-street surveys. Participative techniques (such as community street audits) and more qualitative approaches (such as focus groups and urban design appraisals and workshops) were also employed.

The investigation found that the three case study streets had much to offer their local populations, though they varied in their retail mix. Tooting provided the most comprehensive array of shops and services that opened during the day and into the evening, with a strong Asian component and two off-street markets. Ball Hill catered for a mainly daytime clientele, with few evening activities, whereas in London Road there was a strong evening economy based around pubs and restaurants, and less emphasis on daytime activities.

The link function in all three locations was very important, with high volumes of road traffic and significant numbers of pedestrians 'just passing through' the area, at all times of day. In Tooting in particular, there were also large volumes of bus–bus and bus–underground interchange taking place on the two streets. However, the main pedestrian flows were associated with place-related activities, and in Tooting very high volumes of pedestrian activity were recorded. From the video analysis, 10 different types of place-related pedestrian activity were observed on the footway, ranging from street workers manning street stalls or selling pirated DVDs, to people chatting, resting or waiting for others, as well as small numbers living on the street.[1]

In Tooting and Ball Hill, the main reason for people visiting the street was to shop, whereas eating and drinking were more important in the Sheffield example. The majority of local residents who came to each centre did so on foot – between 80% and 90% in each location. The streets also drew in shoppers and visitors from outside their immediate areas, arriving by public transport or car, and so had a wider, more regional economic and social significance. In general, visitors spent more time and money per visit than local residents, but came to the area less often. As a consequence, while car users spent more money than public transport users or those arriving on foot on a per-trip basis, this difference disappeared when account was taken of the frequency of their visits.

In each location, the local high street proved to be used by all sections of the local population, with a broad cross-section of age ranges and ethnic groups. Patterns of use varied by time and location, reflecting the different lifestyles of the various population groups and the location of different types of business. The only social groups where there were indications of under-representation and possible exclusion were disabled people and people with children in pushchairs. However, the samples were too small in each case to pursue this in more depth.

Both residents and visitors expressed satisfaction with their local high streets in terms of the range and quality of the goods and services they had to offer, and the opportunities for informal social contact they provided. There was much less satisfaction, however, with the experience of visiting these streets as places, and concerns were recorded about the high levels of traffic noise, their poor general appearance, the lack of greenery, and limited and poor-quality amenities such as public toilets and places to sit. The community street audits also identified problems in each location with neglected pavements and messy and cluttered street furniture.

The detailed investigation drawing on CCTV evidence found that the competition for space between the different activities and modes of transport, in effect between various link and place functions, was a source of tension and conflict. In both Tooting and Ball Hill, there were 'pinch points' where pedestrians had to walk on the road when the levels of pedestrian movement were too great for the pavement to accommodate them. Buses were also delayed through lack of adequate pull-in space. In addition to the well-documented problems at road junctions, traffic accidents were concentrated around points of informal public transport interchange, for example, where passengers changed from one bus route to another and crossed the street away from formal crossings.

Crime and antisocial behaviour did not feature as a major problem in any of the case study areas, and it was the overall condition and maintenance of the street that was of more significance to most people. However, it was only in the London example that there was an appointed local authority town centre manger, whose brief was to care for the condition

---

[1] Includes those people in emergency bed and breakfast accommodation who have nowhere to go during the day, and so inhabit the street.

of the shopping centre as a whole. In each area, maintenance and improvement activities were hampered by a lack of powers and the divisions of responsibilities between agencies.

In conclusion, this study has found that mixed-use local high street streets are well used and well liked, and encourage sustainable and inclusive patterns of living. Their potential as significant public places has been hampered by the priority that has been given to their through traffic or link functions, over the needs of people who visit them as places for a variety of purposes. Resolving the challenges posed by the problems and tensions experienced on current mixed-use streets is no small task, but doing so could result in these streets becoming a cornerstone for future sustainable communities.

The report concludes with a series of policy and practice recommendations under four broad headings: adopt a balanced 'link and place' approach to mixed-use street planning and design; provide better coordination between agencies and street-user stakeholders; encourage enhanced information gathering and sharing; and provide more resources and powers.

Introduction

Overview

Currently, mixed-use development is enjoying something of a renaissance in the UK, in academic and policy debates if not yet widely in practice. Definitions of mixed use encompass a broad set of contexts (Coupland, 1997) and suffer from a lack of precise definition. The term mixed use is normally understood to include a range of types of development, from 'broad grain', large footprint buildings of different uses sitting side by side, to the type of 'fine grain' development that incorporates buildings of comparatively narrow width with different uses configured both vertically and horizontally.

This study focuses on the 'fine grain' scale of development. It turns the spotlight on the urban mixed-use street – the traditional high street, outside of the main town or city centre, where a mix of retail, business and public service uses are intermingled with residential dwellings, either above or in close proximity. While city centres have received new funding and new initiatives over the past decade, inner-suburban and district centres in poorer neighbourhoods have been somewhat overlooked. In addition, from the point of view of academic investigation, the street itself has received little attention in the UK as an entity that includes all the activities and attributes that exist there, in terms of movement, local economy, social interaction and townscape. This study aims to fill that gap. Using case studies, it discovers a great richness and diversity of activity, both economic and social, on these streets that has not previously been fully recognised and documented.

It concludes that the traditional mixed-use high street has been overlooked and undervalued by both of the major custodians of key parts of the street – the traffic engineer and the town planner. The reasons why this type of development has suffered from neglect are various and include changes in intellectual approach, professional divides, and societal and economic changes of a more profound nature, such as moves to out-of-town development. Yet most urban mixed-use streets have adapted and prospered. This report contends that they have a key role to play in the future in contributing to achieving urban sustainability, liveability and social inclusion objectives, and that they provide a role model for the development of new sustainable communities.

The remainder of this chapter reviews the literature on mixed-use streets and the wider debates and trends that have influenced their image and development. The chapter concludes by introducing a key concept for analysis: the tension between the function of the street as a 'link' for movement of all kinds and its qualities as a 'place', that is, a destination and an important public space in its own right. Chapter 2 summarises the aims of the study and the wide range of methods employed, provides further definition to the type of mixed-use street investigated and outlines the three case study sites.

The second part of the report presents our main empirical findings. Chapter 3 provides an outline of what the three case study streets have to offer, as important links in the transport system, as local high streets with their commercial and public services and as focal points for local social interaction. Chapter 4 then documents the great variety of use that is made of the case study streets and the extent to which they serve their local communities. Chapter 5 explores in more depth the views of the different groups that make use of the study street. Chapter 6 investigates the conflicts and problems to be found in these high-intensity spaces, particularly in the competing demands for space in their functions as links and places.

Finally, Chapter 7 reviews the findings of the research and suggests that the local high street, as an exemplar of the mixed-use street, provides a model for urban development in the 21st century. The report concludes by considering the issues that face such streets and makes a series of recommendations that require concerted action across a wide range of government and private sector agencies.

Why have mixed-use streets been neglected?

To understand why mixed-use streets have been largely ignored and undervalued for decades, it is first necessary to look at some of the intellectual, economic and social drivers that have influenced transport and planning policies, and urban design.

Modernist approaches to urban development

The impact of modernist ideas on post-war architecture, urban design and planning was far-reaching, for the approach meant that each street would be assigned a specific function, and buildings would be clearly separated from – rather than fronting on to – traffic thoroughfares. This separation between buildings and highways fundamentally changed the character of streets in each urban context where development took place. The spatial qualities of traditional streets were eroded as architectural attention was transferred to buildings as sculptural objects standing in their own curtilage, often with little relationship to the street in front of them or to their neighbouring buildings. This design philosophy transformed streets from acting as continuous 'corridors' defined by their building frontages to becoming a movement artery experienced by vehicle occupants and pedestrians as a progression of different types of spaces, many of which seemed bleak and hostile in practice.

The segregation of the city into functionally distinct zones of living, work and leisure also split apart the complexity of traditional mixed-use neighbourhoods. In neighbourhoods where there was substantial residential redevelopment, traditional mixed-use high streets that depended on these housing catchments for their survival suffered from loss of customers, neglect and economic decline; for example, Crown Street in the Gorbals in Glasgow and Stretford Road in Hulme, Manchester. Although rebuilding did eventually provide new residents and customers, it was too late to save many existing commercial operations. Frequently, traffic engineers had redesignated the street and its catchment area, and taken measures to speed up the traffic passing along it, further damaging the street's economic prospects.

Yet, even as post-war reconstruction based on modernist principles gained widespread acceptance among new generations of built environment professionals, its preconceptions were beginning to be questioned by critics and social commentators such as Jane Jacobs (1961) and William 'Holly' Whyte (1980, 1988). Their observations of the richness of street life enabled them to distil the qualities of good city streets. These qualities were quite simple and, among other design features, included a mixture of land uses accommodated in building frontages at street level. Jacobs and Whyte challenged the modernists' championing of free-flowing space and argued instead for the more traditional form of a street defined by continuous building facades, providing a clear delineation between public and private space and a sense of enclosure.

The publication of *Traffic in Towns* (Buchanan, 1963) provided further challenges to the traditional street. Even though the attitude of the report towards streets remained ambiguous, it became better known for introducing the concept of the separation of people from traffic, using the analogy of 'rooms' (environmental areas) and 'corridors' (traffic arteries), in which the traditional high street had no place.

Few developments were built that included such a complete and thoroughgoing separation of traffic and pedestrians, but nevertheless, the desire for separation and its justification were pervasive. Furthermore, the separation between traffic and pedestrians was not one where each was an equal partner, but a relationship whereby motorised vehicles were accorded preference. The clearest expression of this design ethic is evident in the City of London redevelopment of that time, where pedestrians were relegated to overhead walkways, or subways, accessible by stairways.

A counter-movement was provided by pedestrianisation schemes, many of which were introduced in the 1970s and 1980s (OECD, 1974). These were heralded as pioneering examples in the creation of a traffic-free environment, but were often surrounded by the restricting collar of a high-capacity ring road that cities such as Birmingham are now breaking through at considerable expense.

Car dominance

Desyllas (2006) ascribes the origins of the dominance of traffic over pedestrians to the British Road Traffic Acts of the 1930s, which gave priority to vehicles. However, recent historical investigations by Ishaque (2006) have identified similar tendencies further back, in 19th-century legislation and regulations, where vehicle needs were given precedence over those of pedestrians.

In post-war Britain, new urban roads were also engineered for safety and speed, again with more detailed attention being paid to the needs of the driver rather than the needs of the pedestrian (Hebbert, 2005). Where 'improvements' were required to existing streets, the approach adopted was to superimpose on to existing streets new junctions, roundabouts and other highway forms whose function was to enhance traffic flow. Safety arguments also provided the reasoning for containing pedestrians on the footway, by constructing a system of guardrails and carefully engineered crossing points. This approach to road engineering was enshrined in guidance from central government, for example, in the *Design Manual for Roads and Bridges* (Highways Agency, 1994). While the needs of the driver were carefully thought through, pedestrians tended to be offered only a footway (pavement) of dubious quality and their freedom of movement was severely restricted. Street lighting was directed on to the carriageway rather than the footway, and the copious street signage was designed for motorists driving at speed.

Car ownership grew rapidly in the latter half of the 20th century. Its impact on the traditional high street was felt not only through increased traffic volumes, streets that were re-engineered to cope with these volumes and increased parking pressures, but also through the erosion of many traditional functions of the streets themselves. Retail development, commercial activities and leisure pursuits have all been affected by changes in the urban landscape that car use has supported and encouraged; for example, in the development of large superstores, retail warehouses and office developments set back from the road and surrounded by car-parking spaces.

Out-of-town development and the retail 'revolution'

Changes in UK planning policies in the 1980s permitted an expansion of out-of-town developments that included superstores, hypermarkets, leisure parks and complete shopping centres. The trend towards out-of-town development was reversed in the late 1990s through changes in planning policies, particularly in Planning Policy Guidance Note 6 (DoE, 1996), which required developers to undertake a sequential test to prove that their proposed scheme could not be accommodated within existing towns. Nevertheless, by the time this policy was able to influence development, many town centres and suburban high streets were already suffering competition from, and loss of customers to, these alternative retail sites.

It is not only out-of-town development that has undermined traditional retailers. The 'retail revolution' (Batty, 1997) also relies on the economy of scale that improved communication systems can support, such that 'chain stores' or 'multiples' flourish and come to dominate. Most independent retailers operate at a small margin of profitability, and any small change, stimulated or natural, can price them out of existence quite quickly. In such cases, they are frequently replaced by chain stores, whose scale of activity and ability to pay higher rents has an adverse impact on the viability of independent businesses. Investment in the retail sector has been concentrated in major shopping centres. Diversity in the size and scale of retail activity has also suffered through reductions in the scope of the informal economy, with outlets such as traditional market stalls finding themselves phased out of new developments (Wrigley et al, 2002).

Professional fragmentation in the management of urban areas

In common with that of most streets and public spaces, the management of mixed-use streets and the overall responsibility for their planning and design is highly complex and fragmented. Recent research studies, for example, English Heritage (2000), Baxter et al (2002), ICE (2002) and Carmona et al (2004), have explored aspects of this issue, basing their argument on surveys, case studies and practical experience.

Carmona and colleagues' (2004) report, *Living Places*, sets out the various powers, duties and interests that different stakeholders have in streets and public spaces. The term 'stakeholders' encompasses a broad range of individuals, organisations and agencies. These include private developers (who may occupy a spectrum of power and influence from the individual building owner to transnational public limited companies), businesses, public agencies such as the police, various departments in local government, regional government and central government and organisations representing local communities. All reports highlight the 'silo' mentality that exists in some local authorities, where each department looks to its own scope of activities and practice, without reference to others.

Although the 'silo' mentality is destructive in that, say, cheap maintenance can disfigure the appearance of a high-quality pavement, or measures taken to speed through traffic might reduce the number of potential shoppers, as Davis (1996) points out, public authorities do not set out to vandalise places. Rather, the intellectual traditions from which different officers have derived their working practices vary to such an extent that it is a challenge to understand the others' aims and priorities.

The government recently addressed these gaps between disciplines and practices in the creation of the Academy for Sustainable Communities, which has launched a major study into skills strategies. Alongside this, interdisciplinary working and the expansion of the skills base of built environment professionals is currently being pursued in a number of ways, from well-established courses to in-house training by local authorities and private consultancies.

Education and training are long-term processes and the challenges thrown up by this professional fragmentation remain. Figure 1.1 sets out the manner in which the street is commonly 'zoned' or designated by different professional agencies, using appropriate technical terms that differ from the everyday vocabulary of street users. For example, here the term 'highway' includes the 'pavement' and the 'road', the 'street' includes the building frontage and the term 'footway' is used for pavement.

Figure 1.1: Different components of the street

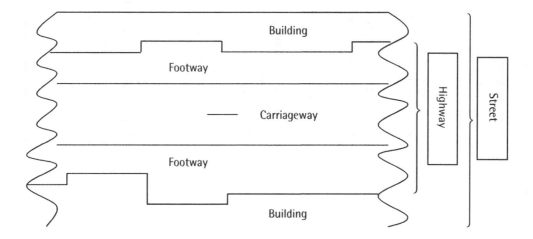

Table 1.1 illustrates the types of responsibility that different arms of local, regional and central government, and various private sector owners and organisations, exercise over the various parts of the street shown in Figure 1.1. This may be read alongside more detailed but partial documents, such as the *Summary of Key Local Authority Public Space Powers and Duties* produced by DEFRA (see Carmona et al, 2004: Annexe C).

The allocation of responsibilities and functions between stakeholders is complex and varies geographically. As in other areas of governance, central government issues directives and guidance notes, some of which are mandatory and some discretionary, for local and regional tiers of government. The implementation of responsibilities may be shared in different ways, depending on the task. Responsibility may lie between different tiers of government and statutory agencies or between the public and private sectors, or be subcontracted wholly to the private sector. Local government itself has different tiers of responsibility inside and outside of London, with splits between district and county councils outside of London, and the boroughs and the GLA in London.

Within authorities, generic activities may be dispersed across different departments. For example, 'planning' is not a monolithic function and includes different departments whose responsibilities may vary from the statutory, such as development control, to the discretionary, such as economic development.

Which authority has responsibility for which street is also an issue. For example, in London, the major traffic routes on the Transport for London Road Network are the responsibility of Transport for London (TfL), whereas the boroughs are responsible for all other streets. Since TfL also controls the London Traffic Signals Unit, and has to be consulted over changes to roads of strategic importance, these together extend TfL's responsibilities for traffic far beyond its own routes.

Table 1.1: Responsibilities associated with different parts of the street

Attribute	Component*	Responsibility
Economic development	Street (road, pavement and buildings)	Local authority
Air quality		Local authority
Planning (strategic)		Local authority/regional planning authority/transport authority
Landscaping (including benches and lighting)		Local authority/transport authority
Crime reduction and prevention		Police/local authority/Crime and Disorder Reduction Partnership
Cleansing	Highway (road and pavement)	Local authority
Signage (road signs, traffic signals)		Local authority/transport authority
Highway management (strategic)		Local authority/transport authority
Stalls (including trading licences)	Footway (pavement)	Commercial owners/local authority
Private forecourts		Private/commercial owners
Advertising boards (licenses)		Local authority
Removal of obstructions		Police/local authority
Maintenance (pavement)		Local authority/utility companies
Phone boxes		Utility companies
Bus stops and shelters		Transport authority
Waste removal	Footway and building (pavement and building)	Commercial owner/local authority
Advertising on building		Commercial owner/local authority
Security (door staff, taxi marshalls)		Commercial/private owners
Design and development (buildings, shop fronts)	Building	Private owners/local authority
Maintenance of buildings		Commercial/private owners
Traffic management	Carriageway (road)	Transport authority/local authority
Parking		Transport authority/local authority
Public transport		Transport authority/private sector
Cables (electricity/phone)		Utility companies
Drainage		Local/regional authority

* Everyday terms shown in brackets.

This situation of divided responsibility is replicated outside London, where certain highway-related responsibilities are split between county- and district-level local authorities, and the Highways Agency. This adds another layer of complexity to understanding how streets are managed.

Policy vacuum

In spite of the complex web of activity in streets, as urban policy developed in the latter part of the last century, mixed-use streets were treated as a legacy of the past and so they have been somewhat neglected in policy terms. After the Second World War, new developments were built first in new towns and settlements, then in out-of-town locations and, more recently, in town and city centres. Planning policy guidance provided direction for the thrust of new development, at first encouraging and then resisting development outside existing settlements. Similarly, transport guidance has focused on highways and residential streets, with no documents explicitly addressing the complexities of mixed-use, local high streets. Even the much heralded draft version of 'Manual for Streets' (manualforstreets.org.uk) focuses primarily on residential streets in new developments.

It is only recently that government attention has started to be paid to the mixed-use street, although official guidance is still lacking. Local high streets remain as one of the many 'layers' of urban development that have persisted throughout the past century and a half. Just as this study has reached completion, the Commission for Integrated Transport (2006) has published a research study that investigates the relationship between retail spend, the mode of transport and retail location. Its advice to the government is that planning policy should support 'a network of small local retail and leisure services, linked to centralised services', a formulation that gives a pivotal role to mixed-use local high streets that are situated on major transport links.

Mixed-use streets re-evaluated

Urban design

While developers were concentrating on constructing out-of-town shopping malls and suburban housing estates, a counter-movement was developing among academics, practitioners and the wider public. The Urban Design Group, a loose coalition of practitioners, academics and interested individuals, set out to challenge the established planning orthodoxies of land-use zoning, and to promote the importance of the public realm. Both the virtues of traditional mixed-use development were extolled (Tibbalds, 1992) and the deficiencies of street scene management and design highlighted (Cullen, 1971). The campaign for better-quality urban design was first taken up by central government in the early 1990s (DoE, 1995), and reached a fuller expression in the report of the Urban Task Force (DETR, 1999). This report argued that the 'dense and varied rhythm of the traditional street' carried 'the quality of mix and variety, the "fine urban grain" of the city that contributes to street life and vitality' (p 50). Referring to them as the vital "glue", the report goes on to add that 'the traditional street plays a key role in the formation of community' (p 57).

High-quality urban design has moved to a key position in government planning policies and is encouraged in *Planning Policy Statement 1* (ODPM, 2005) and the practice guide, *By Design* (DETR and CABE, 2000). Although urban design is still seen as the responsibility of planners and architects by government, and much of the effort to improve public space has been focused on city centres, there has been some movement towards attempting to link urban design principles more directly to street design. In 1998, *Places, Streets and*

Movement was published by the then DETR (Department for Environment, Transport and Regions), as a companion guide to *Design Bulletin 32: Residential Roads and Footpaths* (DETR, 1998) in an attempt to readjust the balance in official guidance towards other matters in street design.

Academics and professional bodies both furthered the cause of streets. Hass-Klau's (1999) study, *Streets as Living Space*, demonstrated the variety of activities that streets accommodate and investigated deficiencies in contemporary practice. URBED's (1994) study of town centres provided evidence for the importance of a comfortable pedestrian environment in traditional town centres. A report hosted by the Institution of Civil Engineers and supported by the Urban Design Alliance, a coalition of professional bodies, argued for an improved, more integrated approach to street design and management (ICE, 2002). The Commission for Architecture and the Built Environment, CABE, which is a quasi-governmental agency, has more recently taken an interest in streets. It has conducted surveys and commissioned reports that delineate the problems faced in achieving streets that the public finds attractive and pleasant (CABE, 2002; Desyllas, 2006).

The benefits of mixed-use streets are gradually becoming recognised. These interests are fuelled by the current government agenda for increasing sustainability, liveability and social inclusion.

Sustainability

In the UK, both Conservative and Labour governments have produced strategies for achieving sustainable development. Along with these, a review of progress towards the achievement of sustainable development is annually published under the title of *Achieving a Better Quality of Life*. Besides the nationally constituted Sustainable Development Commission, the Department of Environment, Food and Rural Affairs' Sustainable Development Unit, and the Department for Communities and Local Government, are both involved in defining, implementing and monitoring the strategy.

The strategy operates at a broad scale. At the local level, definitions of sustainability are harder to derive within the relatively limited context of a mixed-use street. Barton et al (2003), in their manual for new sustainable neighbourhoods, propose a reinvention of the mixed-use high street. Their argument for its sustainability as a focus for local retail and commercial uses is based on the catchment area for a residential neighbourhood enabling local residents to walk or cycle to the facilities. This provision of local services that are accessible by pedestrians or by those taking public transport fulfils wider sustainability objectives.

However, the failure experienced by many district centres in redeveloped housing developments, when cut off from wider transport networks, suggest that these retail centres can only maintain economic viability when they are easily accessible from outside the neighbourhood and can draw on a wider population for custom (Duany, 2003; Allen et al, 2005). In this regard, traditional mixed-use streets, which are often located on the former radial streets leading out of town and city centres, may prove to be more sustainable than were purpose-built district centres constructed in the geographical centre of housing estates.

Increasingly, issues of 'sustainability' have become permeated with the rising concerns of central government with liveability and social inclusion. These concepts encompass notions of environmental quality, access and social equity.

Liveability

Lucas et al (2004) have observed a clear difference emerging between what is now referred to as 'doorstep' environmental concerns and the wider issues of sustainability. The MORI survey of 2002, *The Rising Prominence of Liveability* (Page et al, 2002), found that a majority of the people questioned judge the fabric of real life based on what is immediately around them, and that local perceptions of quality of life turned out to be quite different from the national definitions. The survey also found that, in areas where local authority standards had fallen in terms of maintaining the street scene through cleaning, making improvements and so on, there was an increased local dissatisfaction with liveability.

Liveability thus emerged strongly as a local agenda issue, one endorsed equally by central government. CABE, in association with MORI (2002), established a strong correlation between liveability and public spaces. Following the Urban Green Spaces Taskforce report (DTLR, 2002), the government's programme for improving the quality of public spaces and local environments was set out in *Living Places – Cleaner, Safer, Greener* (ODPM, 2002). Highlighting the decline in the quality of public space services, and the need for investment to tackle the legacy of dereliction and backlogs of repairs, the publication proposed the objective of creating high-quality public spaces that catered to the diverse needs of communities, providing access to all. What was also stressed was the need to combine good planning and design with effective management and maintenance to make the places more attractive, cleaner, safer and, most importantly, sustainable in the long term.

This association between liveability and public spaces had already been established when the Office of the Deputy Prime Minister launched the Sustainable Communities Plan in 2003. In this plan, liveability was identified as a key ingredient, involving efforts to improve the local environment of all communities through cleaner streets, improved parks and better public spaces. A new Liveability Fund was introduced with a list of suggestions that included improvements to parks, gardens, sport pitches and playgrounds; general measures on public space design and traffic calming; street cleaning and streetscape issues, such as litter and waste disposal, abandoned cars, graffiti, fly tipping, fly posting, dog fouling, street furniture, lighting, pavement repairs and noise; and general safety issues.

But many of the substantive elements of sustainable development are not covered by – and are beyond the scope of – the liveability agenda. Eames and Adabowale (2002) have raised the question of whether liveability and its emphasis on locally led and driven environmental action can improve social cohesion and generate social capital.

Social exclusion

Social exclusion occurs when people or places suffer from a combination of problems such as unemployment, discrimination, poor skills, low incomes, poor housing, high crime, ill health and family breakdown. In Britain, there has been increasing concern about concentrations of poverty and its 'area effects' (SEU, 2003). Such concentrations of deprivation place excessive pressure on public services, and are associated with higher levels of crime and disorder and a reduction in private sector activity (Berube, 2005). Limited attention has been paid specifically to mixed-use streets, but academic scrutiny has been directed towards social exclusion – and its converse, inclusion – in public spaces.

Critical attention has been directed towards the extent to which public space can become a setting in which people of diverse backgrounds come together, with an opportunity to observe and become familiar with others whose appearance and habits are alien to themselves, in an atmosphere of mutual tolerance (Gehl, 1996). With regard to residential areas, Gans (1968), in critiquing Jacobs (1961), argued that people wanted 'quiet privacy'. Anderson (2004), in contrast to Jacobs' account, portrays streets as places where pedestrians move about carefully, encountering strangers with careful degrees of eye contact and gestures in order to maintain 'impersonal but private zones for themselves'. For him, anonymous pedestrians 'see but don't see' one another. Thus, 'more subtle modes of exclusion are woven into much deeper class and cultural interpretations of whom a place is "for"' (Atkinson, 2003, p 1832). The extent to which traditional mixed-use streets can act as 'social glue' remains open to debate and is empirically unproven.

Whatever suspicions are cast on mixed-use streets, their existence stands in strong counterpoint to the highly controlled and privatised spaces of shopping malls and leisure parks. A number of studies have made the point that traditional high streets in urban areas perform a significant role as spaces of social inclusion (see, for example, Zukin, 1995; Hebbert, 1998). By contrast to shopping malls, high streets offer open access 24 hours a day, without private security guards acting as 'gatekeepers' to entry or setting standards for behaviour that conform to the desires of the private landowner. Nevertheless, tensions between the objectives of liveability, sustainability and social inclusion provide an introduction to further tensions and conflicts that are associated with the regeneration and refurbishment of mixed-use streets.

Mixed-use streets: regeneration and renaissance

Regeneration, gentrification and consumption

In the 1980s, while out-of-town development gained momentum, as has already been noted, there was the beginning of a shift back to the urban, mixed-use environment for city centre redevelopment, based on the benefits of proximity of amenities that city centres offer. Critics have been quick to observe that this regeneration is in fact a form of gentrification by professional, high-income wage earners, spawning what Zukin (1995) calls 'domestication by *cappuccino*'. As has also been noted, the trend for out-of-town retailing was challenged by the adoption of *Planning Policy Guidance Note 6*, or PPG6 (DoE, 1996). Town centre management has also emerged as an activity and this, too, has been retail-led. For the 21st century, retail-led urban regeneration has become a successful means of bringing economic life and vibrancy back to many locations (CABE, 2004).

While retail is clearly the most high-profile town-centre use, the question of how much space it allows for other uses needs to be addressed as well. The domination of retail in land use raises concerns at different levels. In many deprived areas, local shopping centres – with their community facilities, libraries, surgeries and pubs – are at the social and physical heart of neighbourhoods, as many residents are among the almost one third of British households without a car. While the current replacement of PPG6, the new *Planning Policy Statement 6* (ODPM, 2006), recommends that planning authorities include a range of activities in their town centres, there is still guidance in favour of maximising the most profitable retail and leisure uses.

Commercial leisure uses have become particularly pertinent with the unforeseen expansion of a 'night-time economy' of bars, restaurants and nightclubs. While the arguments in favour of expanding evening and night-time uses were drawn from Jacobs (Bianchini, 1995), their 'hijacking' by the corporate power of entertainment companies (Hollands and Chatterton, 2003) has led to many high streets becoming 'demographic ghettos' (Mintel, 2004), catering for 16- to 24-year-olds after dark. The violence and disorder associated with youthful drinking has reinforced the tendency for older people to avoid town centres at night (Bromley et al, 2003). Local authorities have been relaxed about a proliferation of night-time venues in some instances, because it has provided 'regeneration on the cheap', but they now recognise that the negative externalities involved have created a new order of problems (Roberts, 2004).

Crime and security

Among the most potent arguments for mixed-use streets is that of crime prevention. Jacobs' (1961) account highlighted the by now well-known concept of 'eyes on the street' that extends from when the first shop opens during the day to when the last bar closes at night. These ideas have been adopted as key tenets of contemporary urban design and this approach is also favoured by the government (Home Office and ODPM, 2003). Continuous street frontages with 'active' ground floor uses and occupied upper stories provide 'natural surveillance' for the street, which through functional diversity is continuously 'peopled' throughout the day and most of the night. Yet this approach to 'crowding out crime' is not without its problems. Hillier (2004) points out that in crowded streets, street crime tends towards pickpocketing in contrast to the more serious assaults that tend to occur in back alleyways and less populated streets.

Jacobs' view of street retailers as 'great street watchers and sidewalk guardians' (Jacobs, 1961, p 46) is now regarded as rather romanticised, as the nature of retailing and trade on the street had been radically transformed since her time, with the advent of corporate chain stores and managers who are moved on at regular intervals. Some critics have voiced concerns about the levels of social control in major retail-led urban renaissance. In some instances, this has produced a zero-tolerance policing policy, with crackdowns on aggressive begging and the imposition of child curfews (Atkinson, 2003).

This is not to suggest that crime, disorder and antisocial behaviour are not significant issues. Numerous studies have highlighted their negative effects on property, individuals and groups. Older people and women are deterred from entering certain streets and spaces due to crime and fear of crime. Yet it is young males who are most likely to be the victims of violent, unprovoked assault (Pain, 2001). The way in which space is perceived can itself be exclusive and, if fear of crime reaches a certain level, this in turn has a negative impact on property values.

Efforts to prevent crime are equally subject to criticism for being exclusionary in nature. Policing tactics have been scrutinised for their acceptance of privatisation, whether by private security guards or through the privatisation of spaces (Raco, 2003). In the UK, CCTV is used routinely to provide policing and surveillance. The efficacy of CCTV has been challenged, with the crime prevention charity Nacro (Armitage, 2002) providing evidence that the provision of better street lighting leads to a higher level of reduction in crime. Nevertheless, a dilemma remains. Atkinson (2003) comments that 'a thorny question remains over whether some degree of exclusion is a necessary price for policies which seek to secure public space and maintain a wider quality of life' (p 1829).

New approaches to the public realm

During the lifetime of this study, a new integrated approach to street design has emerged that argues that it is the urban street as a place that is important, rather than pavements simply being there as an adjunct to the through-route of the vehicular carriageway. This view demands a reappraisal of most aspects of the design of the highway, from signage, through lighting to junction layout. Current assumptions about safety have also been overturned, with the argument that accidents are reduced when drivers are forced to take account of potential hazards, such as pedestrians unexpectedly stepping in their path, rather than being insulated from them.

An alternative approach to reappraising the functions and values implicit in street design was initially pioneered by Appleyard in the 1970s (Appleyard, 1981). His observations that social interactions among residents were reduced on heavily trafficked residential streets have received international recognition (de Vasconcellos, 2004). Appleyard demonstrated that increased volumes of traffic act as dividers in residential streets, cutting neighbours off from each other. He recognised the inherent conflicts and contradictions that are played out in the design and management of different types of street.

New approaches to reconciling pedestrian comfort and traffic management have emerged from the Netherlands. The pioneering work of Hans Monderman has demonstrated that a new relationship between pedestrians and motorists may be forged through the concept of 'shared space' (Shared Space, 2005). This concept recognises that drivers will not willingly harm pedestrians. Monderman found that driver behaviour changes fundamentally where there are visual clues about the nature of the carriageway and the likely hazards. These visual clues do not take the form of road signs or conventional traffic calming humps, but are integral to the design of the street itself (Hamilton-Baillie and Jones, 2005; Engwicht, 2005).

Kensington High Street in London provides an example of this type of new approach to street design. Here it was only with the leadership and personal guarantees of an elected councillor that an integrated design could be attempted. Guardrails were removed, signage redesigned and simplified, and the footway improved dramatically. Close attention was paid to the quality of the pedestrian environment and the street as a public space.

This integrated approach is not without its own paradoxes and tensions. For example, activities that Gehl (1996) categorises as optional and social often require elements on the street such as furniture, cafes, benches and sitting areas to encourage socialising and provide spaces for them; but this means that crucial space for pedestrian movement is taken away and may be compromised. Or, where ground floor units have to be shuttered for safety and security reasons, they create a sense of insecurity for the pedestrian on the street (Gehl Architects, 2004). Disabled people have also queried whether 'shared space' is suitable for visually impaired pedestrians.

Link and place

A further refinement to approaching streets both as places for economic and social activity and as arteries of communication has been developed by Jones et al (2007), building on the work of the EU ARTISTS project (www.tft.lth.se/artists). Mixed-use streets perform a wide range of functions that can be broadly grouped under the primary headings of 'link' and 'place'.

As a link, the mixed-use street is a higher-level road in an urban-wide network, distributing general traffic within and beyond the urban area; it may also form an important section of a strategic public transport bus or tram network. Link functions are catered for on the mixed-use street by providing traffic lanes for vehicle movement, possibly with priority lanes for certain methods of transport (for example, bus or cycle lanes), and associated street furniture (for example, traffic signals and direction signs). Footway space also provides an important connection for pedestrians passing through the area.

As a place, the mixed-use street is an important attractor and destination in its own right, usually offering a broad range of retail and other commercial services, as well as a range of public services that form a focus for local communities. Place functions mainly occur in the buildings and forecourts along the street, and on the pavement. Vehicle parking and loading is also a place-related activity, much of which is catered for in the carriageway space.

The ways in which the mixed-use street is used are many and varied, and can broadly be regarded as being associated with either the link or place functions of the street: Link users comprise drivers of cars, vans, buses, taxis and HGVs, motorcyclists, cyclists and (some) pedestrians. Place users and uses include buildings and associated businesses, employees, shoppers, residents, visitors, vehicles parking and loading. Place users also need to access the street themselves. Most user groups require a certain amount of space to carry out their activities, and user needs are likely to vary over time. For example, weekdays are likely to differ from weekends and daytime hours differ from the night-time, and activities also vary by location along the street.

Conflicts may be anticipated between different aspects of engagement in the street, which are broadly of two types (Jones et al, 2007). The first consists of *competition* for space or capacity. This includes competition for carriageway space, between buses and cars, or loading and general traffic; and competition on the footway, for example, between street sellers and people in a hurry. The second type is that of *compatibility* constraints: even where sufficient space exists, some street uses may not be able to coexist comfortably; for example, fast traffic and pavement cafes, or buses and cycles on high-speed routes.

The concepts of link and place provide a conceptual framework for examining a key set of tensions within mixed-use streets. The pioneering investigations of Whyte (1980, 1988) and Appleyard (1981), discussed earlier, explored similar issues of incompatibility and competition in a US context. This study provides an opportunity to explore all these issues and tensions in a contemporary UK context, focusing on the street as an entity.

Summary

This chapter has taken as its definition of mixed-use streets the urban district centres that are essentially high streets on main roads running through residential areas outside of main town centres that incorporate business and retail use. The chapter has explained the reasons why the link functions of mixed-use streets have for the past 50 years been given priority over their place activities and functions, resulting both from an over-emphasis on the link connection by traffic engineers and an under-emphasis on place by town planners, in this context. Conflicts and tensions between link and place have resulted, and have been largely resolved in favour of the link function to the detriment of the pedestrian environment and its ambience.

When modernist approaches to urbanism were in the ascendancy, such streets were either neglected or were subjected to inappropriate re-engineering that took the enhancement of traffic flow as its main priority. A campaign for high-quality urban design, combined with a new focus on sustainability, provoked a re-evaluation of mixed-use development as beneficial. Mixed-use streets, as defined here, are often located in more deprived areas and consequently these streets offer the possibility of fulfilling government objectives as socially inclusive places within the context of sustainability that places priority on pedestrian movement and activity.

In order to do so, issues of liveability, street design and management have also to be addressed. These are complex issues and involve a plethora of agencies and actors. In addition to the tensions and conflicts already noted between traffic and pedestrians and agencies and actors, the enterprise of street improvement raises concerns about gentrification, social control and social exclusion. Further, improvements to the public realm may cause tensions and conflicts between different styles of engagement with the street, for example, between the activities of sitting and socialising, and walking and shopping.

This study started from the position that although, paradoxically, mixed-use streets have been treated as a legacy of an outdated form of urbanism, they actually contain lessons for the future development of cities. Much that is known about the way in which they function is derived from texts that were written decades ago, on another continent. There is now a pressing need to understand these streets in a British context: what they are, how they work and how they might be improved. This study sets out to fill these gaps in our knowledge.

Study objectives and methods

2

Objectives

The previous chapter set out the case for investigating the circumstances of contemporary British mixed-use streets, arguing both that they are undervalued and largely unrecognised. For the purposes of this study, they are defined as being high streets, on main traffic routes running through residential areas outside the main town or city centre, with a mixture of shopping, business and public service uses, and residential dwellings either on higher floors, intermingled with other uses or close by.

This study has the overall aim of attempting to build a picture of how these high streets function and are managed, what views the different stakeholders hold of them, how the tensions and conflicts manifest in their operation are articulated and what improvements could be made. This is in the broader context of considering their potential contribution to addressing national concerns about sustainability, liveability and social inclusion.

The specific objectives outlined for the research were:

- to identify the range of actors with an interest in mixed-use streets, their perceptions, attitudes and concerns;
- to investigate the conflicts in different aspects of mixed-use streets: the complexity of their various functions and the fragmentation in their management;
- to examine the qualities of mixed-use streets as places, rather than just as thoroughfares for traffic, and how they might be improved;
- to examine the hypothesis that mixed-use streets form a model for sustainable urban development;
- to develop conceptual and analytical frameworks that assist in analysing the tensions and conflicts inherent in mixed-use streets; and
- to propose recommendations for the future development of mixed-use streets.

The case studies: criteria for choice

Because mixed-use streets are varied and complex, and have not been intensively studied in the past in a comprehensive manner, a case study approach was used in order to meet the objectives of this research. Resources permitted a study of three mixed-use streets, of different scales, in different geographical locations. The narrowing of the definition of mixed-use street to the concept of an inner-urban high street, with a particular emphasis on studying deprivation rather than wealth, assisted in locating suitable case studies.

There were four criteria for the selection of the case studies, as follows:

- **Good land-use mix:** at the heart of a district centre, providing the main focus of the area's retail and leisure facilities; multiple retailer representation and smaller independent stores.
- **Key transport corridor for public and private transport:** a major road carrying several bus routes along that corridor, possibly including an underground, tram or train station.
- **High degree of deprivation:** social exclusion was one of the issues chosen for investigation, to see what role mixed-use streets might play in contributing to or ameliorating the problem.
- **Strong project partnership:** because of the broad range of data needed, it was preferable to build on any data already collected for the case study street through pre-existing schemes, such as a bus improvement scheme, or an ongoing district centre survey. Such cooperation enabled the project to build up a larger and more comprehensive dataset than resources would have otherwise permitted, and helped to establish contacts in the business, residential and professional communities.

Using these criteria, mixed-use, inner-urban high streets were selected as case studies in Coventry (Ball Hill), South London (Tooting) and Sheffield (London Road). Again, because of their complexity, only the core sections of the streets could be subjected to rigorous scrutiny.

General comparison of the case study streets

This section sets out a general comparison of the three case study streets. Ball Hill in Coventry, located to the east of the city centre, is the smallest of the three sites, with a total length of around 420 metres and 106 commercial businesses. It is a district centre on a major radial route, with several small multiples and branches of most high street banks. It has been highlighted by the council as having particular air quality problems, and was in the process of being examined as part of a corridor bus priority scheme.

Table 2.1: Ball Hill – essential features

Length of road	420m
Number of shops	106 – district centre
Deprivation	Cuts across areas that feature in the bottom 15-20% of the most deprived areas in England, and also secured funding from the European Regional Development Fund and the Single Regeneration Budget
Traffic volume (weekday, 08.00-19.00)	10,400 vehicles
Bus routes	10
Buses per hour (weekday, 08.00-19.00)	43

Tooting in South London is the largest of the three case studies, by a considerable degree, being a major district centre; it contains around 350 shops and businesses, including two major off-street covered markets. Two streets were included in Tooting, representing two arms extending from the major Tooting Broadway junction, where there is a Northern Line underground station. In all, nearly 1,800 metres of streets were examined in the case study, to varying degrees.

Table 2.2: Tooting – essential features

Length of road	1,790m
Number of shops	365 – major district centre
Deprivation	Surrounding wards are 13% more deprived than the average wards in England and 17% more deprived than the average wards in the borough (Wandsworth). The borough itself is seen as a transitional authority, previously attracting Single Regeneration Budget funding.
Traffic volume (weekday, 08.00–19.00)	14,800 vehicles on Mitcham Road, 17,000 vehicles on Upper Tooting Road
Bus routes	10 on Mitcham Road, 3 on Upper Tooting Road
Buses per hour (weekday, 08.00–19.00)	159 on Mitcham Road, 58 on Upper Tooting Road

The third site, London Road in Sheffield, is intermediate in scale between Tooting and Ball Hill. It contains around 130 businesses over a length of 770 metres, and lies on a radial route to the south of Sheffield city centre, feeding into the inner ring road. Unlike the other two sites, it has very few multiple chains and has a strong focus on food and drink outlets, and the night-time economy. At the northern end of the site is a large, free-standing Waitrose supermarket, adjacent to the inner ring road.

Table 2.3: London Road – essential features

Length of road:	770m
Number of shops	129 – district centre
Deprivation	Contains areas that feature in the 15% most deprived wards in England
Traffic volume (weekday, 08.00–19.00)	13,500 vehicles
Bus routes:	5
Buses per hour (weekday, 08.00–19.00)	63

All sites included residential areas within close proximity.

Looking more closely at Tables 2.1-2.3, it is evident that:

- daily vehicle two-way traffic flows (08:00 to 19:00) range from 10,400 vehicles in Ball Hill, to 13,500 in Sheffield and 17,000 on the busiest section in Tooting;
- buses per hour range from 43 in Ball Hill to 63 in London Road up to 160 on the busier road in Tooting;
- both Ball Hill and London Road are surrounded by wards in the bottom 15%-20% of deprived wards in England, while Tooting is below the average for the London Borough of Wandsworth.

The remainder of this chapter describes each site in turn, in greater detail.

Ball Hill, Coventry

East of Coventry city centre, the area of Ball Hill centres on Walsgrave Road on the A4600, which heads east out of Coventry to meet Junction 2 on the M6 and M69. Ball Hill is one of the three major district retail centres in Coventry. Its shops are in the possession of many independent owners. There are a few major chains or multiples, and the centre features the majority of the major high street banks. The location and layout of Ball Hill is shown in Figure 2.1.

Figure 2.1: Ball Hill case study area

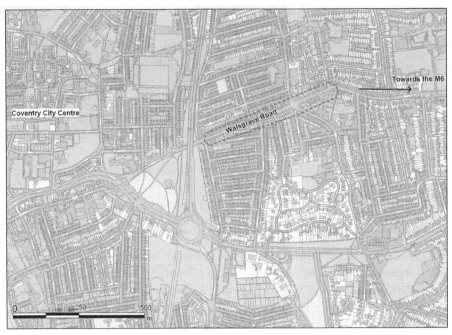

Ball Hill was developed at the turn of the last century, before the First World War. The case study section of street is flanked mainly by two-storey shop-houses, of Victorian style and suburban scale. The study area includes two portions of Walsgrave Road, separated by the junction of Clay Lane and Bray's Lane. The shops congregate on either side of this junction.

Ball Hill – national retailer

Ball Hill – independent stores

The hill itself rises to a peak to the west of the junction and from this height the centre of Coventry is just visible and the spire of the cathedral can be glimpsed. The most visually interesting buildings are in this portion of the street, the most prominent being the Old Ball, a historic pub. Two-storey, brick terraced housing predominates in the hinterland of the street, punctuated by some industrial premises. The housing is configured in a grid of long narrow blocks. Vehicular permeability to the high street is blocked on three of the residential streets leading off Walsgrave Road.

Ball Hill has only one significant pub and most of its restaurants do not open in the evening. This is probably because the night-time economy uses are concentrated in Far Gosford Street further west along the corridor, adjacent to the city centre and close to the university. The lack of an evening or night-time economy, combined with the predominantly low scale of building, give the centre a suburban ambience.

Walsgrave Road was chosen as a study site because the road was designated by Coventry City Council as an Air Quality Management Area, that is, as an area with severe air quality issues that the council is obliged to resolve; the city council is both the highway and the planning authority for the street. In addition, the council is in the process of introducing a bus corridor improvement plan (PrimeLines) along the street, which initially proved to be contentious with the local traders' association. These two initiatives provided some data and consultation that the project team could draw on.

Tooting, South London

Tooting was fully developed as a suburb in south-west London between the end of the 19th century and the First World War. It lies within the London Borough of Wandsworth. The study area chosen was nearly twice the size originally envisaged because it incorporates the two major shopping streets that form the arms of an 'L' that branch off from Tooting Broadway underground station, as shown in Figure 2.2. These are the A24 (Upper Tooting Road) and the A217 (Mitcham Road). Both roads are significant because they form part of the major radial and arterial route network across London.

Figure 2.2: Tooting case study area

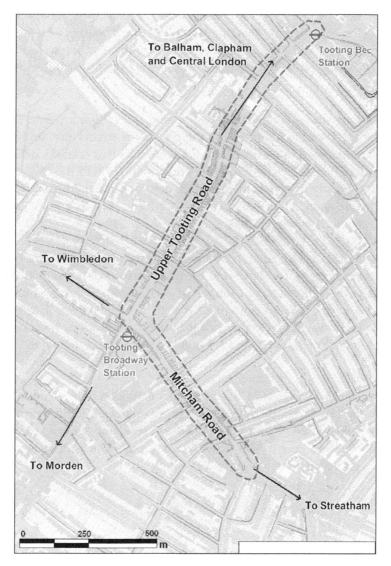

The land use on the two roads is quite distinct, with a concentration of shops selling ethnic goods and services on Upper Tooting Road and more multiples around the Broadway. There is also a small concentration of pubs and bars on Mitcham Road.

Tooting Broadway junction

Upper Tooting Road

The character of transport networks on the two roads is quite different. Upper Tooting Road is a Red Route forming part of the Transport for London Road Network (TLRN), owned and managed by Transport for London (TfL), and has three bus routes, with an underground station at both ends (Tooting Broadway and Tooting Bec). Mitcham Road is a major borough road and a major bus corridor carrying 10 different routes, some of which feed into Tooting Broadway station, and serve a large hospital nearby (St George's Hospital).

In terms of built form, the predominantly two-storey, late 19th-/early 20th-century terraced housing that characterises the hinterland to the case study streets has barely changed. These terraces are arranged in narrow, long grids of roads that connect directly to the case study streets. The upper storeys of many buildings fronting on to the two study area streets have not changed greatly in appearance either. They vary in height from two to three storeys and there are some larger buildings of distinction, such as a grade 2 listed former cinema that is now used as a bingo hall.

Over the years, there has been some redevelopment, with larger footprint buildings such as a Primark supermarket and a Marks and Spencer store constructed near the Tooting Broadway junction. The most recent example of such development is an imaginative juxtaposition of a new Sainsbury's supermarket with a college above it, adjacent to Tooting Broadway underground station. Despite being a suburb of London, Tooting has an urban character, due to the close packed massing of its built form and the height of many of the buildings.

Tooting has an active Town Centre Partnership that is funded by the London Borough of Wandsworth and led by a very proactive town centre manager. In the partnership, business and community stakeholders, such as the police and residents' groups, meet and decide how to improve the town centre. This provided the study team with some initial base data, in conjunction with information about the TLRN held by TfL.

London Road, Sheffield

London Road (B6388) is situated directly south of the inner ring road (A61) around the centre of Sheffield, parallel to Bramall Lane where Sheffield United has its football ground. It used to be the main traffic route into the city centre from the south, but there is now an alternative route for through traffic.

The junction of London Road and the ring road at St Mary's Gate is marked by a major office development on the city centre side. The original intention was that pedestrian access would be through the office development from London Road on a straight line directly into the city centre. Regrettably, the tenant for the office development is currently insisting that the ground-level pedestrian access under the building be blocked for security reasons, so a substantial detour is necessary. In addition, an underpass forms the main pedestrian access across the inner ring road between London Road and the city centre.

The orientation and layout of the case study street is shown in Figure 2.3. The road is known as a food and drink destination, primarily oriental food, and there are takeaways and other night-time economy uses throughout its length. Apart from the supermarket adjacent to the ring road, there are no other large multiples on the street. There are specialist shops and commercial services. At the southern end of the case study portion of the street, where it forks, there is a cluster of distinguished 19th-century buildings, many of which are now devoted to public, community or commercial uses. The pressure for student housing means that many of the flats over the shops are inhabited.

London Road – looking south from
the inner ring road

High density residences
close to London Road

Of the three case study streets, London Road has experienced the most dramatic changes to the residential streets that feed into it. The two-storey terraced houses on its western side suffered severe war damage and have been replaced by a series of tower blocks, accessed by pedestrian paths and dedicated vehicular drive-ins for each block. A portion of the terraces on the eastern side has been replaced by one-storey housing for older people, and new student accommodation is under construction.

Figure 2.3: London Road case study area

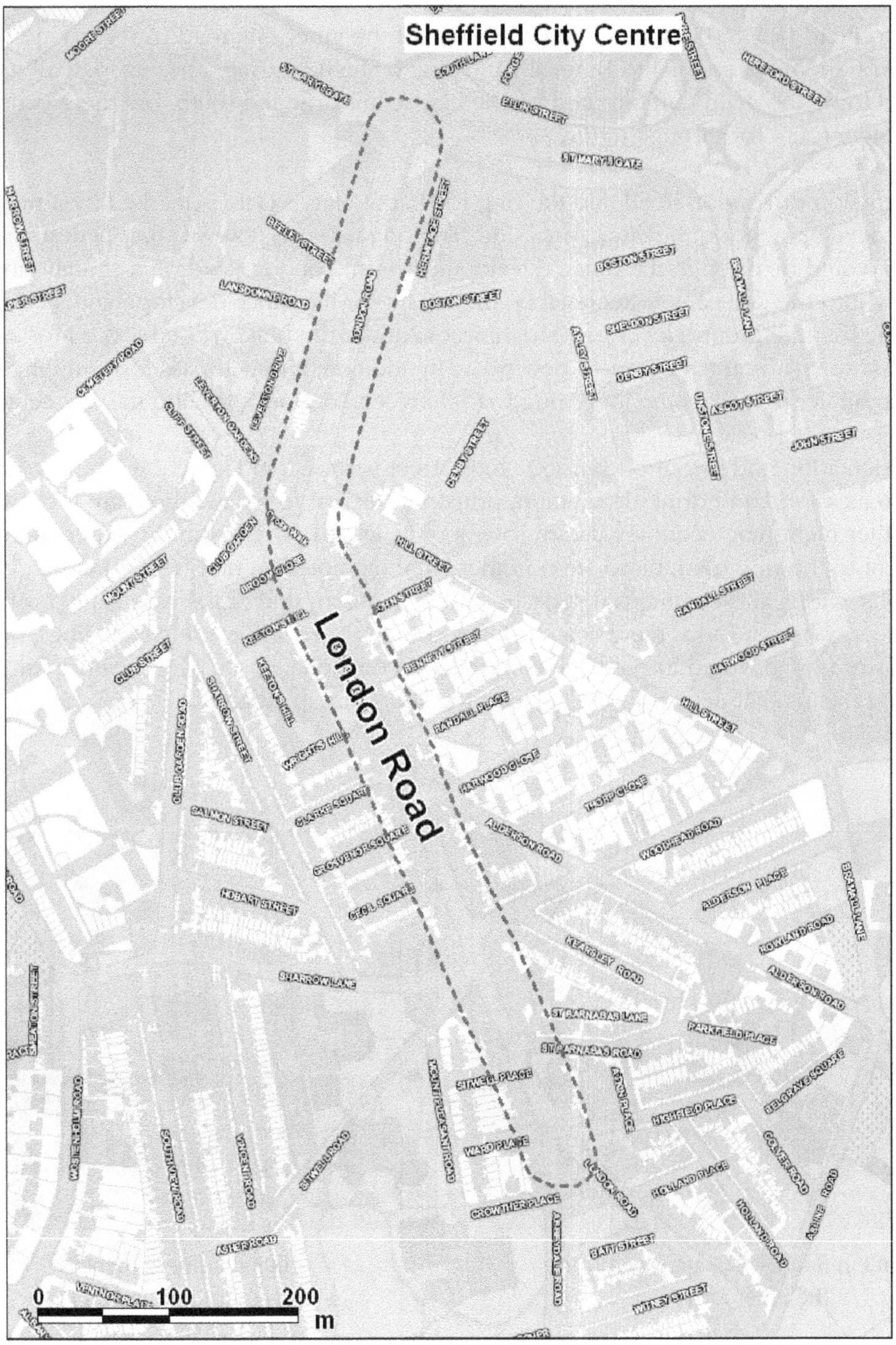

Source: Ordnance Survey.

Sheffield City Council is the local authority responsible for London Road. The road cuts through the area of Sharrow, which comprises some of the most deprived output areas in the country. While regeneration funding has gone into the area as a whole, London Road has never been seen as a priority in itself. There is no traders' association. However, a local community organisation, the Sharrow Forum, has drawn up a programme of schemes that aims to enhance the area's status within Sheffield. Creating a business forum is one of the initial steps in the programme, as part of an overall aim to develop the creative and economic potential that has been neglected in the area over the years. London Road is very much a focal point within this vision for the area.

Methods

Due to the range and complexity of the issues that were being explored in the three case study areas, eight broad approaches to data collection and analysis have been employed, as described below.

Collating existing data

Given the wide range of assets and activities on mixed-use streets, there is a broad and diverse range of existing data, in different formats, that summarises this information. Examples of such data collated and used in this study include:

- land-use types
- business rates and council tax bands
- vehicle flows
- public transport usage
- parking facilities
- street furniture
- street crime
- traffic accidents.

These data were used to build up a picture of how mixed-use streets function.

Urban design analysis

Each case study area was subject to a detailed urban design analysis that covered:

- building form and uses
- permeability (degree of connectivity to the local street network)
- legibility (extent to which the streets have a strong visual identity)
- axonometric (3-D) representation
- street sections
- potential pedestrian and visual conflicts.

The urban design analysis explored the characteristics of the streets as places. It enabled a more detailed analysis of the connections between the streets and their residential hinterland to be made. In the case of Tooting, the analysis was used to form the background to an urban design workshop, in which improvements to the street were discussed with an advisory panel of residents, businesses and statutory agencies.

Community street audits

In two case study areas (Tooting and London Road), a local community street audit was carried out as part of this research. The community street audit method, originally developed by Living Streets, involves active consultation with residents, shopkeepers and business people, by walking through the area with them and examining the issues. At the end of the walk, a discussion is held, drawing out key themes and recommendations that are summarised in a written report. In Ball Hill, the local authority had already commissioned a similar street audit, to which the researchers had access.

In each case, topics addressed included:

- footway surfaces and obstructions
- facilities and signage
- maintenance and enforcement of regulations
- personal security
- crossing points and desire lines
- space allocation
- aesthetics
- general traffic issues.

While the urban design analysis provided a broad overview of the spatial experience of each street, the street audit elaborated the pedestrian experience of the street in more detail. Generally, the area for investigation focused on the footway, the carriageway and the shop fronts. The street audit was able to log the neglect of the street and to pin point where there was particular street furniture clutter.

Street video analysis

Video surveys were carried out on two of the streets in order to examine the variety of footway and carriageway uses in greater detail. In Tooting, video from existing CCTV cameras was made available by the borough; in Ball Hill, there were no existing cameras, and the council funded a special CCTV survey.

The resulting data comprised:

- Tooting: 24-hour coverage, for a Thursday, Saturday and Sunday.
- Ball Hill: coverage from 08.00 to 19.00, on a Thursday and a Saturday.

A variety of analyses were carried out, including;

- vehicle counts, by vehicle type and direction;
- turning movements at key junctions;
- pedestrian counts, along the footway, by direction and numbers of wheelchairs and pushchairs;
- pedestrian crossing movements, formal and informal, by direction and numbers of wheelchairs and pushchairs;
- pinch points affecting movement along the footway;
- observation of activities carried out on the footway;
- use of footway as a public space.

This video material enabled movement along the streets to be counted and compared for different times of day and days of the week. This provided valuable information about the link functions of the streets. It also provided useful evidence for the place function of the streets, including the use of street amenities, such as seating. Most usefully, it provided evidence of conflicts, as, for example, when buses blocked traffic movements, or when pedestrians walked in the carriageway because of congestion on the footway.

Stakeholder surveys

Face-to-face interviews were carried out with three groups of people with a strong interest in the case study streets. Because of the different scales and temporal dynamics of the three streets, the numbers and timing of those interviewed varied between each one. The groups included:

- Businesses along the case study streets:
    - 150 businesses were surveyed in Tooting (44% of the study area businesses);
    - 78 in Ball Hill (80% of the study area businesses);
    - 87 in London Road (54% of the study area businesses).
- Residents living within one kilometre of Tooting and London Road:
    - Tooting: 309 surveyed in total, split into two areas;
    - London Road: 207 surveyed, split into 4 different residential areas;
    - no residents' dwelling-based survey was carried out in Ball Hill, as the council had recently conducted a similar survey here.
- People walking along the case study streets:
    - Tooting: total of 512 street users. Approximately 100 were interviewed on each street during the day, on a weekday and on a Sunday, with a further 100 interviewed on Mitcham Road in the early evening.
    - Ball Hill: 489 street users in total. The street was split into six sections and interviews were divided equally over these sections, on both a weekday and Saturday daytime.
    - London Road: 405 street users overall. Three sections were marked out and all three were sampled over both a weekday and a Friday/Saturday night.

The three surveys probed for information both about street perceptions and behaviour. Each differed in detail, but had many common elements, including:

- reason for using the street;
- method of transport used to reach the street;
- expected time and money expenditure that day;
- satisfaction with local business services;
- satisfaction with provision of public facilities and street condition;
- concerns about traffic and personal safety and security;
- characteristics of the respondent or their business;
- suggestions for improvements.

Focus and design groups

Focus groups were carried out with local residents and business representatives in the Tooting area, and design workshops were carried out in Tooting and in Ball Hill. In London Road, informal discussions were held with local residents and stakeholders in the course of a local community event.

The focus groups, workshops and informal discussions helped to enrich the information gathered from other sources. These qualitative encounters could begin to probe feelings and attachments to the streets, providing an indication of their emotional effect. They also revealed some underlying tensions between different groups. Respondents were also able to voice their hopes and fears for the future of the streets.

Professional interviews

This strand of the research sought to identify and interview people from a selection of the key agencies and organisations, mainly in the public sector, with an interest in some form of asset or activity on the case study mixed-use streets.

The interviews were carried out face to face, or by telephone, and addressed issues such as:

- interviewee's role, remit and powers;
- service issues and problems;
- links with other agencies in the study area;
- any areas or overlap of confusion with other agencies.

Ten interviews took place among professionals with street-related responsibilities (for example, in planning, design, construction, operation, management and enforcement) in Tooting and in London Road, and 13 were undertaken in Ball Hill.

The interviews enabled the team to probe the arrangements for the planning and management of the case study streets, and to assess where gaps, tensions and conflicts were occurring. They also revealed incidences of cooperation.

Data analysis and presentation

A wide variety of forms of data analysis have been carried out, both quantitative and qualitative. Wherever possible, these have been linked into a common GIS (geographical information system) database for each case study area.

The results have been presented in a variety of ways in the remainder of this report, including:

- maps
- drawings
- photographs
- figures
- tables
- quotations.

Comparisons have been made at various points between the three case study sites, drawing on the wealth of information collected.

Summary

This chapter has set out the aims and objectives of the study, which seeks to investigate the characteristics, operation and tensions that coexist on mixed-use, inner-urban high streets. The three case study streets in South London, Coventry and Sheffield show commonalities in terms of basic functions and areas of difference with regard to their specific operations, commonalities that this study sets out to explore. The study uses a wide range of methods to capture the richness of each street's function and life.

In drawing all the analyses together, the next four chapters provide a unique comparative picture of life on the three mixed-use streets, in the period 2004-05. This will enable us to draw out conclusions regarding the contribution that such streets make towards liveability, sustainability and social inclusion, and to explore the tensions between the various link and place functions inherent in mixed-use streets.

What do mixed-use streets offer users?

Mixed-use streets are both important links in the urban road-based transport networks and, at the same time, places of economic and social importance for the community. Therein lies their uniqueness.

As links: key components of the transport system

Parts of strategic networks

Each case study street performs a vital function as a primary route within the transport and movement systems for their urban area. This function also supports their existence as local high streets, as places with good access by a variety of methods of transport.

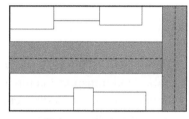

Link space in the street

Traditionally, mixed-use streets grew up on major routes into city centres, which provided high levels of passing trade to augment the custom provided by residents living within the local catchment area. The link function is thus an important aspect of mixed-use high streets.

Figure 3.1 shows Tooting's location. The centre provides key links at the intersection of two major routes, one from the south coast to central London (A24), and the other forming an important tangential link between inner south and inner west London (A214). Both are also important bus corridors.

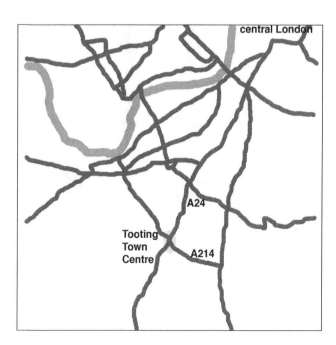

Figure 3.1: Location of Tooting at a strategic road intersection

Ball Hill is similarly strategically located to the east of Coventry city centre, as a link on the main trunk radial route (A4600) between the M6 (and, indirectly the M1) and M69, and the city centre. As can be seen in Figure 3.2, it also lies on a major bus corridor to/from the centre of Coventry.

Figure 3.2: Location of Ball Hill on a strategic bus corridor into Coventry

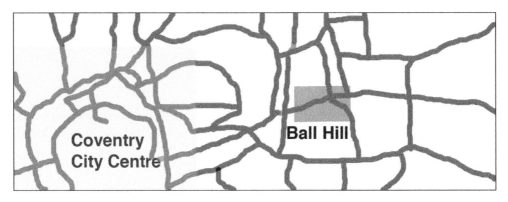

Transport interchanges

Within each of the case study mixed-use streets are embedded transport interchanges, accommodating movements between different methods of transport, often at key junctions. Typically, these streets cater for bus-to-bus and walk-to-bus interchange, but in the case of Tooting interchanges also occur between bus and underground services. This results in four patterns of modal interchange, as shown in Figure 3.3.

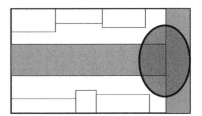

Interchange space in the street

Figure 3.3: Possible interchanges between different transport modes in Tooting

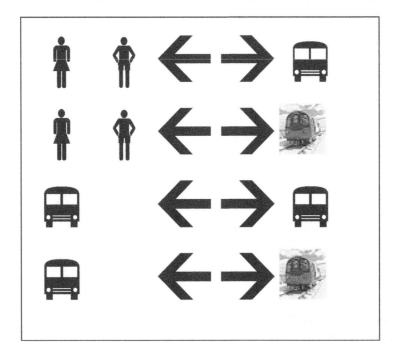

Local catchment area networks

The street networks surrounding the case study mixed-use streets play an important role in channelling people on to the high street. Their configuration strongly influences the mixed-use streets' catchment areas, both for those arriving on foot and those travelling by bus or by car. This catchment area function can be systematically analysed using an urban design technique known as 'permeability analysis'. This provides a visual representation of the number of paths and routes that might be taken through an area to reach one destination. The analysis is carried out by marking on a street map vehicular and pedestrian routes and observing their patterns. Generally speaking, the easier a street is to reach by a variety of pedestrian routes, the greater the likelihood that it will flourish economically (Hillier, 1996).

A comparison of the patterns for each of the case study streets (Figures 3.4 and 3.5) demonstrates that Tooting has the largest and most permeable catchment area for both pedestrians and vehicles. By comparison, London Road is the most restricted: the housing area to the east of London Road has cul-de-sac driveway entrances that restrict movement beyond that development. Similarly, the area to the south, around the school and community buildings, has no east–west connections.

Figure 3.4: Permeability diagrams for Tooting and London Road in 2005, demonstrating the contrasting multiplicity of routes

Source: derived from Ordnance Survey.

Conditions in the Ball Hill area are intermediate between the other two. The main street is severed by the Clay Lane/Bray's Lane cross-route, which restricts east-west permeability to the north. Three of the side roads that feed on to Walsgrave Road have been blocked for vehicular transport, but provide good pedestrian access.

Figure 3.5: Permeability diagram for Ball Hill in 2005, showing crossroad and junctions blocked to vehicular traffic

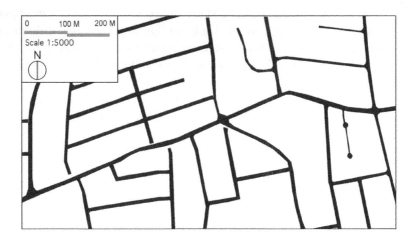

Source: derived from Ordnance Survey.

One way of quantifying an aspect of permeability is to count the number of side-road and footpath entries to each mixed-use street on both sides per 100 metre length of main street, distinguishing where appropriate between vehicle access and pedestrian access, and well-connected routes and poorly connected ones. The appropriate rates for each case study street are shown in Table 3.1.

Table 3.1: Number of entry points to each mixed-use street per 100 metres

	Tooting	Ball Hill	London Road
Total access points per 100m (including pedestrian only routes)	2.12	1.83	2.75
Car access points per 100m	2.01	1.00	2.50
Access points well connected into catchment area per 100m	2.12	1.78	1.50

When considering the total number of entry points per 100 metres, London Road has the highest number (2.75), followed by Tooting (2.12) and Ball Hill with the lowest number (1.83). If pedestrian-only access points are excluded, the figures for car access drop slightly in Tooting (from 2.12 to 2.01) and on London Road (from 2.75 to 2.50), but nearly halve in Ball Hill, from 1.83 to 1.00. However, if cul-de-sacs and similar streets that do not extend substantially into the residential catchment areas are excluded, the total number of entry points in Tooting and Ball Hill remain largely unchanged, while on London Road they drop by 45%, from 2.75 entry points per 100m to only 1.50 per 100m, making London Road the least permeable of the three sites. This matches well with the visual patterns of permeability shown in Figures 3.4 and 3.5.

As places: important centres of commercial and public services

Diversity of street frontage activities

Mixed-use streets offer a wide range of retail and service activities, both public and private, and attract a range of businesses, from multiple chains to small independent suppliers. Each street has its own unique character, however, reflecting both local geographical and historical factors (Chapter 2), and local market conditions.

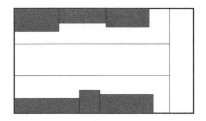

Frontage space in the street

The three case study streets illustrate the richness and diversity of the provision of goods and services to be found on British mixed-use streets, both in the adjoining buildings and spaces, and spilling out onto the forecourts. While most of this enterprise focuses on providing daytime activities, more businesses now cater for the evening and night-time economy. Although, inevitably, more is on offer on the longer sections of mixed-use street, even in the smallest of the centres, Ball Hill, there is a diverse range of provision.

Each centre has its own identity and 'unique selling point': the markets and Asian shops and restaurants to be found in Tooting, the oriental restaurants and take-aways along London Road, and the strong presence of the major banks and local traders in Ball Hill.

Figure 3.6 shows the richness and diversity of what is on offer in the Ball Hill area, and along part of the Tooting case study streets. As well as a broad range of commercial and retail services, all sites feature libraries, several churches, other religious buildings, and various community services.

However, where there is considerable difference to be found between the three case study streets it is in the relative balance of daytime and night-time provision.

While offering a wide range of goods and services, most of the businesses on Ball Hill are open between 09.00 and 18.00. This means that after 18.00 the shutters come down and much of Ball Hill is 'closed' until 09.00 the next day. This creates a slightly bleak and intimidating environment for pedestrians after dark: there are few 'eyes on the street' from busy shops or restaurants, as shown below.

Daytime in Ball Hill

Night-time in Ball Hill

Conversely, while there are some specialist local daytime businesses along London Road (for example, a 'hair philosopher' hairdresser and a spa equipment centre), the predominant form of land use is takeaways and restaurants, most of which open for the evening only. This creates a strange daytime environment along parts of the street, where there are shuttered frontages among the remaining retail outlets, as shown below.

Limited daytime activity on London Road

Many premises on London Road are closed during the day

Figure 3.6: Variety of goods and services in Ball Hill and Tooting

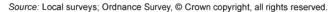

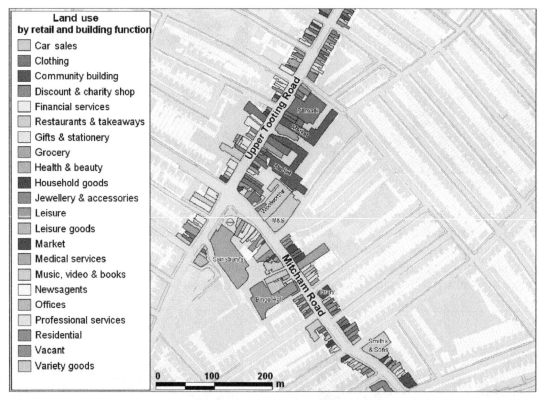

Tooting, by comparison, offers a broad and well balanced mix of businesses and other services, with major stores and the off street markets open during main trading hours, and smaller shops and pubs and restaurants open well into the evening.

Looking down Mitcham Road from
the Broadway junction

Retail activity outside Tooting Broadway
underground station

Varied on-street facilities and services

A wide range of retail and service activities can be found
on the streets themselves, as well as public amenities
and a variety of street furniture that assists in regulating
street activity. Beneath the streets lie the utility pipes and
cables that sustain modern living.

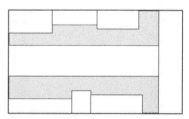

Space for facilities and services
in the street

In addition to a diverse range of frontage activities,
mixed-use streets house different forms of infrastructure
that provide a broad range of services on the street itself,
mostly on the footway. These are wide-ranging in nature,
and include:

- additional retail services, such as market stalls, tobacconists, paper sellers or flower
  sellers;
- communication services, including post boxes, telephone boxes and internet kiosks;
- cash point machines and mobile phone recharging points;
- public transport services infrastructure, including bus/tram stops, timetables, shelters and
  taxi stands;
- marked spaces for parking and loading activities;
- public amenity services, including seating and benches, public toilets, waste bins and
  information points;
- public art, from sculptures to fountains;
- greenery, from hanging baskets to trees.

Facilities for street users

There is also a variety of other forms of 'street furniture' associated with information provision, wayfinding, security and regulation of movement. These include:

- sign posts and road signs;
- advertising boards and A-signs;
- tactile paving;
- parking meters and cycle-parking stands;
- traffic and pedestrian signals;
- bollards and guardrails;
- control boxes, for signals, telecommunications and so on;
- street lighting columns;
- CCTV cameras;
- traffic volume, air quality and noise monitoring stations.

Street furniture that informs or constrains street users

Figure 3.7 shows the range and diversity of street furniture located on the footway along a short section of Tooting High Street, using data extracted from the Transport for London AIMS database.

Figure 3.7: Street furniture in a section of Tooting High Street

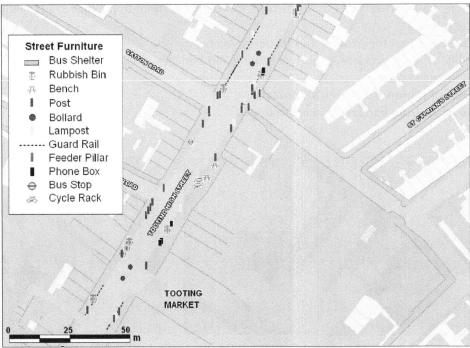

Finally, beneath the surface of the street lie the pipelines and cables of the many utility companies (gas, water, electricity, telecommunications) on which city dwellers depend for their daily life. These are only visible above ground through various inspection hatches and other access points – and when streets need to be dug up to access the pipes and cables.

Major public spaces

Mixed-use streets are important public spaces, providing the backdrop against which people from a variety of social backgrounds and circumstances encounter one other. The construction of isolated buildings breaks the continuity of street facades, undermining the street as an enclosed space. The rediscovery of the attributes of successful public spaces has drawn attention to the value of the conventional mixed-use street layout.

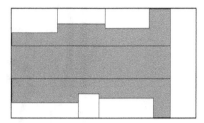

Public space in the street

In considering the degree of enclosure offered by a street, two factors are of critical importance: the continuity of the building facades, and the ratio between building height and highway width.

Continuity of the building facade

If the building facade is not continuous, the street, as a place, disappears. Of course, streets do feed into designed open spaces such as squares, circuses and piazzas, but if a street facade is absent, due to an undeveloped site, for example, the experience of an enclosed, defined space is undermined (Trancik, 1986).

Each of the case studies has continuous street faces for most of its length. This is illustrated by the 'figure ground' plans of the three sites (Figure 3.8), which illustrate the continuity of built form, its size and shape and the spaces between. The buildings are shaded in black and all the other spaces, both public and semi-public, in white. They demonstrate the 'morphology' of the street, that is, its shape on plan, and provide a vivid graphical representation of the relationship between public and private space.

In general, both Tooting and Ball Hill have a continuous building facade along their high streets. By contrast, the northern end of London Road has become fragmented as it reaches the ring road. A sense of dislocation from the city centre is reinforced by the presence of two large free-standing buildings, a supermarket and a major student union and halls of residence building, the Forge. The ill-defined space that surrounds these two buildings destroys the sense of enclosure that is apparent on the remainder of London Road, as shown on the right.

'Gateway' to London Road, looking north, where the definition of the street as a place is lost

Figure 3.8: Figure ground diagrams of the case study streets illustrating continuity of building facades along the street

Ball Hill

0   100 M   200 M   N
Scale 1:5000

Tooting

N   0   100 M   200 M

Scale 1 : 7500

London Road

0   100 M   200 M   N
Scale 1:5000

Ratio between building height and highway width

The second critical factor with regard to enclosure is the ratio between the height of the buildings that face on to the street in relationship to its total highway width, that is, the footway and carriageway combined. The case study streets have varying height: width ratios along their length, but on average the rather suburban ratio of 1:3 for the Walsgrave Road (which reaches 1:4.5 at the junction) may be compared to the more urban 1:2 of Tooting High Road (Figure 3.9).

Figure 3.9: Comparative street sections for Tooting and Ball Hill

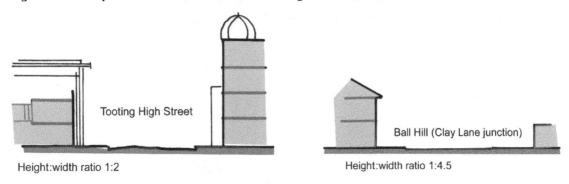

Tooting High Street

Ball Hill (Clay Lane junction)

Height:width ratio 1:2

Height:width ratio 1:4.5

The street section for London Road is influenced by its topography and the sense of enclosure is increased by the gradient (Figure 3.10).

Figure 3.10: Street sections for London Road

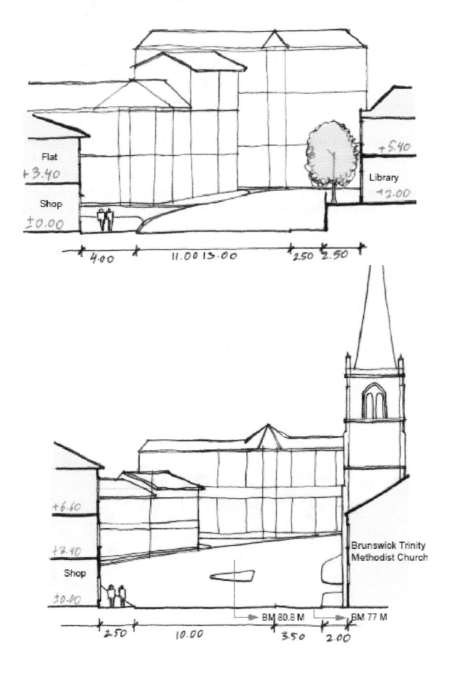

In Ball Hill, the carriageway at the crossroads is so extensive that the proportions of the street do not provide a sense of enclosure, and the continuity of the street across the junction in interrupted.

Expansive area of carriageway at the junction of Walsgrave Road with Clay Lane and Bray's Lane

Although each case study street, with the exception of the fragmented spaces noted above, provides a strong sense of enclosure, each lacks defined public spaces apart from the street itself. There are two exceptions. In Tooting, the widened footway in front of Primark accommodates two benches, as shown in the photograph below. In London Road, there is a small triangular space at the junction with Alderson Road; this also accommodates some seating.

Public space and seating area in Tooting

Landmarks and centres of local identity

Landmarks, in the form of memorable buildings or spaces, are important components of place making, both as a means of orientation for the resident or visitor and as elements of local identity. These were identified, both from the viewpoint of the professional urban designer and from surveys of street users.

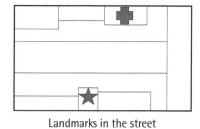

Landmarks in the street

In the street-user surveys among residents and visitors, respondents were asked which were the most familiar features on the high street that helped them orient themselves, and give the area a sense of identity. People were most clearly able to identify and agree on a relatively small set of landmarks in the Tooting survey; elsewhere, responses were more varied and individual.

In Tooting, 35% of the street users who were interviewed identified the underground station as the most familiar feature on the street that helped them identify where they were (Figure 3.11). Other important buildings were the major stores, such as the Sainsbury's superstore, Marks and Spencer and Primark. A minority recognised the bingo hall, which is a grade II listed building. This contrasted with the urban design analysis, where greater emphasis was given to buildings that had an historical association, or a strong physical presence on the street.

Figure 3.11: Tooting street-user responses to the question, 'What are the most familiar features on the street that help identify where you are?'

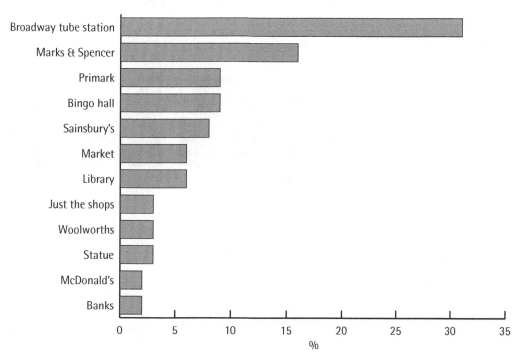

Source: Tooting street-user survey, total sample of 512 respondents.

From an urban design perspective, London Road has a wealth of interesting and distinguished buildings, which provide local identity in their use of local stone, as illustrated in Figure 3.12. However, it was specific restaurants, clubs or pubs that proved most memorable to visitors and residents, and there was much less evidence of a common set of shared landmarks; the most frequently mentioned building was the local library, which was referred to by only 7% of respondents.

In Ball Hill, around one third of respondents mentioned one of the banks or building societies clustered around the major road junction in the centre as their main point of reference. Twenty per cent mentioned the main local supermarket (Kwik Save) and around 12% each for Woolworths and the post office. Only one landmark that was identified as important in urban design terms also scored significantly among respondents; this was the Old Ball pub, mentioned specifically by 17% of respondents.

Figure 3.12: London Road: historic and interesting buildings

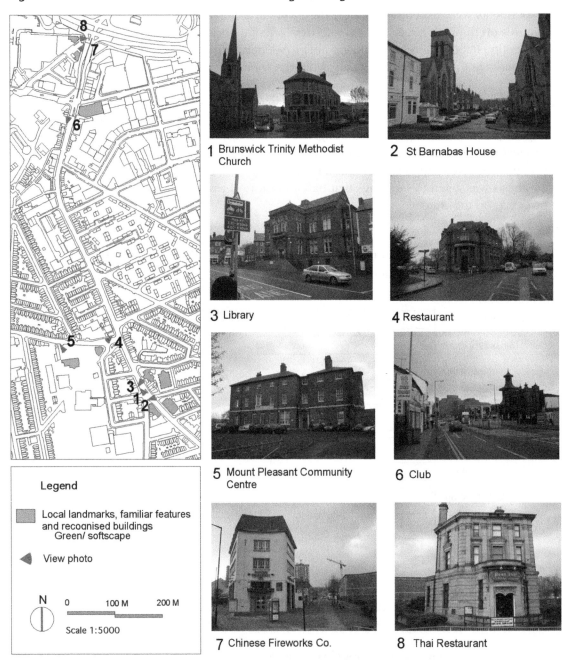

1 Brunswick Trinity Methodist Church

2 St Barnabas House

3 Library

4 Restaurant

5 Mount Pleasant Community Centre

6 Club

7 Chinese Fireworks Co.

8 Thai Restaurant

Legend

Local landmarks, familiar features and recognised buildings Green/ softscape

View photo

N   0   100 M   200 M

Scale 1:5000

Summary

Mixed-use high streets cater for a wide range of link and place functions. Some of these are immediately apparent (for example, the through traffic movement link function), while others are less obvious (for example, providing an important bus–bus interchange space in Tooting). Some of these occupy their own unique spaces (such as land uses within frontage buildings), but most share space with other competing demands. In particular, the footways and carriageway both cater for various movement activities and, within the envelope of the building facades, provide an enclosed public space in which a wide range of other activities take place.

In the next chapter, we look in some detail at the kinds of activity that populate these various street spaces.

4

How are mixed-use streets used?

Mixed-use streets provide a setting in which a wide variety of everyday activities take place. The previous studies reviewed in Chapter 1 have focused on particular street activities, but none has recorded the full range of street users and uses on a section of street. This chapter seeks to remedy this deficiency by documenting the various ways in which the three case study streets were used, drawing on video analysis, existing data and street surveys. It starts by looking at the transport link functions of these streets, and then considers various forms of pedestrian activity, the profiles of street users in general and of the place customers that visit the various businesses on and alongside the mixed-use streets.

Intensity of transport activities

Volumes and characteristics of through movement

Mixed-use streets accommodate large volumes of vehicles throughout the day that are travelling through the area, with little interest in the street itself, as well as substantial numbers of pedestrians who are just passing through.

Traffic volumes

Across the three case study sites, the two-directional traffic volumes over the 11-hour period from 08.00 to 19.00 range from around 10,400 vehicles in Ball Hill (Walsgrave Road) and 13,500 vehicles in London Road, Sheffield, to 17,000 vehicles on each of the main roads in Tooting.

Figure 4.1 shows the total (two-directional) traffic flows on Mitcham Road and Upper Tooting Road, for selected hourly periods and different days of the week. What is especially notable is that the high volumes of road traffic continue well into the night, particularly at weekends. While by 01.00 to 02.00 on a Thursday morning flows are only about 30% of their daytime levels, on a Friday night/Saturday morning and a Saturday night/Sunday morning, they are much higher, at between 50%/70% and 60%/70%, respectively. The higher of the night-time flows are to be found on the radial route to/from central London (that is, Upper Tooting Road).

Vehicle composition

Vehicle composition varies between the three study areas and changes between weekdays and weekends. The predominant vehicle type across all three areas is cars, varying from 70% of the vehicle flow in Tooting on a Thursday to 89% in Ball Hill on a Saturday. In

Figure 4.1: Variations in traffic flow over day and night in Tooting

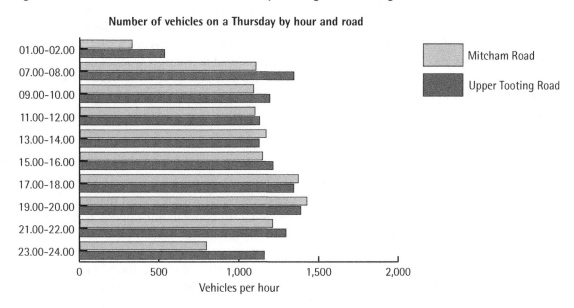

Number of vehicles on a Thursday by hour and road

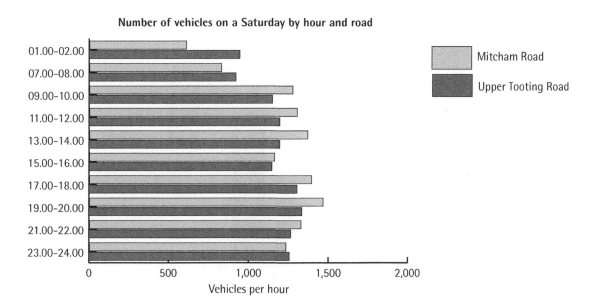

Number of vehicles on a Saturday by hour and road

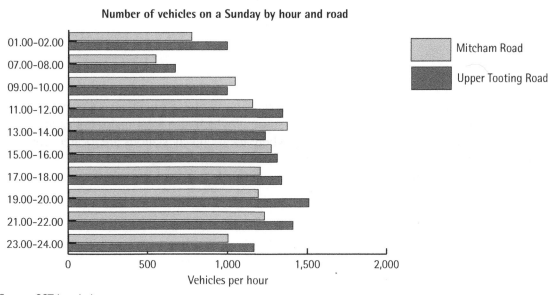

Number of vehicles on a Sunday by hour and road

Source: CCTV analysis.

Ball Hill on Thursday, around 10% of the flow along Walsgrave Road comprises light goods vehicles (LGVs), with heavy goods vehicles (HGVs) forming 2% of the flow. On the Saturday, this drops to around 5% LGVs and a nominal number of HGVs. Buses remain at a constant level of around 5% of flow on both days. Similar patterns are found on the other streets, reflecting the greater concentration of commercial activity on weekdays. In Tooting, there is also a drop in the proportion of motorcycles and pedal cycles at weekends, reflecting a drop in commuting trips at this time.

Pedestrian through movement

The through movement link function is not solely confined to motor vehicle traffic. The on-street surveys found substantial numbers of pedestrians who reported that they were just passing through the area, as shown in Figure 4.2. In general, this applied to a higher proportion of residents than visitors.

The highest proportions of pedestrians passing through the area were found on London Road (30% residents, 25% visitors), perhaps reflecting the more specialist nature of the services on offer there. Only 11% of residents and 6% of visitors were just in transit in Ball Hill, rising to 20% and 10%, respectively, in Tooting.[2]

Figure 4.2: Proportion of on-street users passing through the area

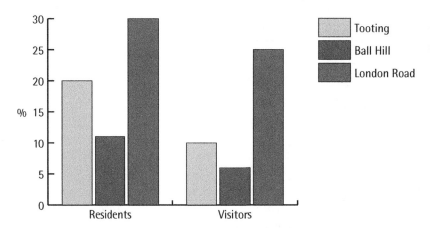

Source: street-user surveys.
Base street users: Tooting = 512, Ball Hill = 489, London Road = 405

Mixed-use streets as transport interchanges

Many of the larger mixed-use streets have grown up at points of high accessibility around major junctions in the urban road network, some of which also form major nodes in the public transport network – particularly where local railway stations are located. As a consequence, there are high levels of informal interchange activity on mixed-use streets that have not previously been well documented. This is explored in more detail here, using Tooting as a case study example.

---

2   Note that the street interviews in Tooting were not carried out in close proximity to the underground station and neighbouring bus stops, where the proportions of pedestrians just passing through the area would be likely to be substantially higher.

Underground passengers

On a typical weekday, around 33,000 people enter or leave Tooting Broadway underground station through its only entrance, adding significantly to the volumes of pedestrian movement in the vicinity of this major road junction.

Figure 4.3 shows the variations in the number of passengers entering and exiting the station on a typical weekday. Given the location of Tooting, it is not surprising that there is a predominance of people entering the underground station in the morning, and leaving later in the day – reflecting the role of the area as a dormitory settlement for employees working in inner and central London.

Concentrating now on the passengers leaving the underground station during the day, Figure 4.4 shows the method of transport next used by passengers. Here we see that, of the total sample (including the 6% who did not answer this question), 63% completed their

Figure 4.3: Number of passengers entering and leaving Tooting Broadway underground station, by time of day

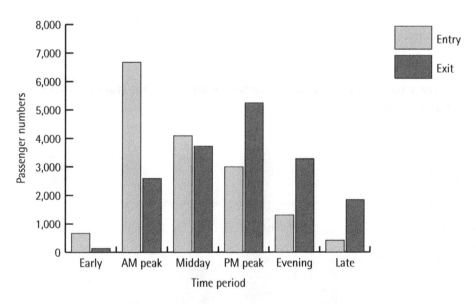

Source: TfL RODS (Rail Origin-Destination Survey) data. Sample size: 16,134/16,804.

Figure 4.4: Method of transport used by underground passengers after leaving Tooting Broadway station

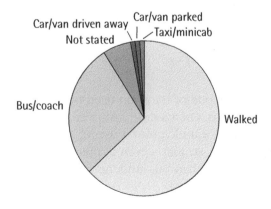

Source: TfL RODS data. Sample size: 16,804.

journey on foot, to local destinations such as homes, workplaces, or shops. Around 30% of underground users had no interest in Tooting as a place, using it simply as a transport interchange: 28% walked to a local bus stop to continue their journey elsewhere, with other transport modes being used by 1% or less of respondents.

Bus passengers

The other major form of public transport in Tooting is the bus. Figure 4.5 shows the number of people boarding and alighting from buses in the Tooting area, within 500 metres of the Tooting Broadway junction on an average weekday. Over an 18-hour period, there are over 46,000 bus passengers who board or alight from buses in this area between 04.00 and 22.00; this is substantially higher than the 33,000 passengers joining/leaving the underground at Tooting, making the bus the primary public transport mode for people travelling to and from the Tooting area.

In contrast to the very different patterns of entry and exit throughout the day at Tooting Broadway underground station, the two sets of boarding/alighting patterns for bus passengers are much more evenly balanced. In addition, average bus passenger flows tend to be fairly evenly spread throughout the day (averaging around 10,000 per three-hour period between 07.00 and 19.00), rather than being concentrated in the morning and evening peak periods as with underground users (as shown in Figure 4.3).

Figure 4.5: Average number of passengers boarding/alighting at bus stops on Tooting Broadway on a weekday

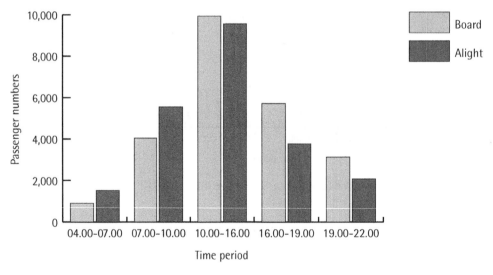

Source: London Buses BODS (Bus Origin-Destination Survey) data. Sample size 46,241.

Finally, Figure 4.6 shows the mode of transport used by bus passengers in the Tooting area after they alight from a bus. On average, just over half complete their journey on foot (a lower proportion than for underground users), 19% switch to the underground and 28% interchange to another bus, so that – even at this busy underground node – bus–bus interchange is about 50% greater than bus–underground interchange.

Figure 4.6: Mode of transport used after alighting from a bus in Tooting

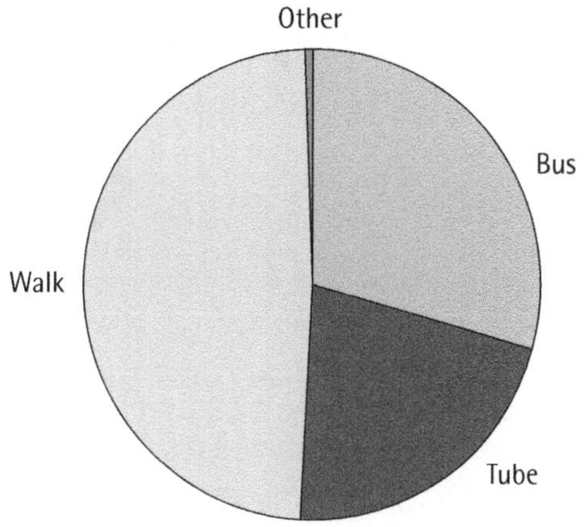

Source: London Buses BODS data. Sample size 46,341.

Bus–underground interchange

The major pedestrian flows between the underground station and adjoining bus stops are illustrated in Figures 4.7a and 4.7b. Most interchanging bus passengers live to the south of Tooting and there is only one station entrance, so this results in large asymmetrical pedestrian movements. Those joining the underground (Figure 4.7a) remain on the same side of the road, whereas those leaving the station (Figure 4.7b) have to cross Mitcham Road to reach the southbound bus stops – thereby generating a large pedestrian crossing movement where the road is very wide and particularly busy. The latter movement tends to be greater, as some people who walk to the station in the morning catch a bus home in the evening

Pedestrian activity on the street

Number of pedestrians using the streets

A key indicator of the vibrancy of place activity on mixed-use streets is the intensity of pedestrian movement, or 'footfall'. This plays a major role in setting retail rents, and in attracting certain types of business to that locality. Volumes can vary quite considerably within a small area, however, due both to the varying attractiveness of the businesses and other local factors, such as locations of car parks and bus stops.

Flows along the footways

Not surprisingly, pedestrian flows are higher in the larger centres. Comparing the smallest and the largest of the case study areas, Ball Hill and Tooting, we find that pedestrian flows along the two sets of footways typically vary by a factor of three on weekdays and four on Saturdays – the busiest day of the week (Figure 4.8).

The highest daytime flows are recorded in Tooting, with around 30,000 pedestrians passing on both sides of Upper Tooting Road on a Saturday and 25,000 on Mitcham Road. Both sets of flows were recorded well away from the Tooting Broadway junction area, where localised flows are likely to reach 40,000 to 50,000 per day. Note that in both these case study areas, flows can be quite different on the parallel footways, reflecting both the relative attractiveness of the land-use activities and the location of car parks, bus stops and underground stations.

Figure 4.7a: Weekday interchange patterns from buses to underground in Tooting

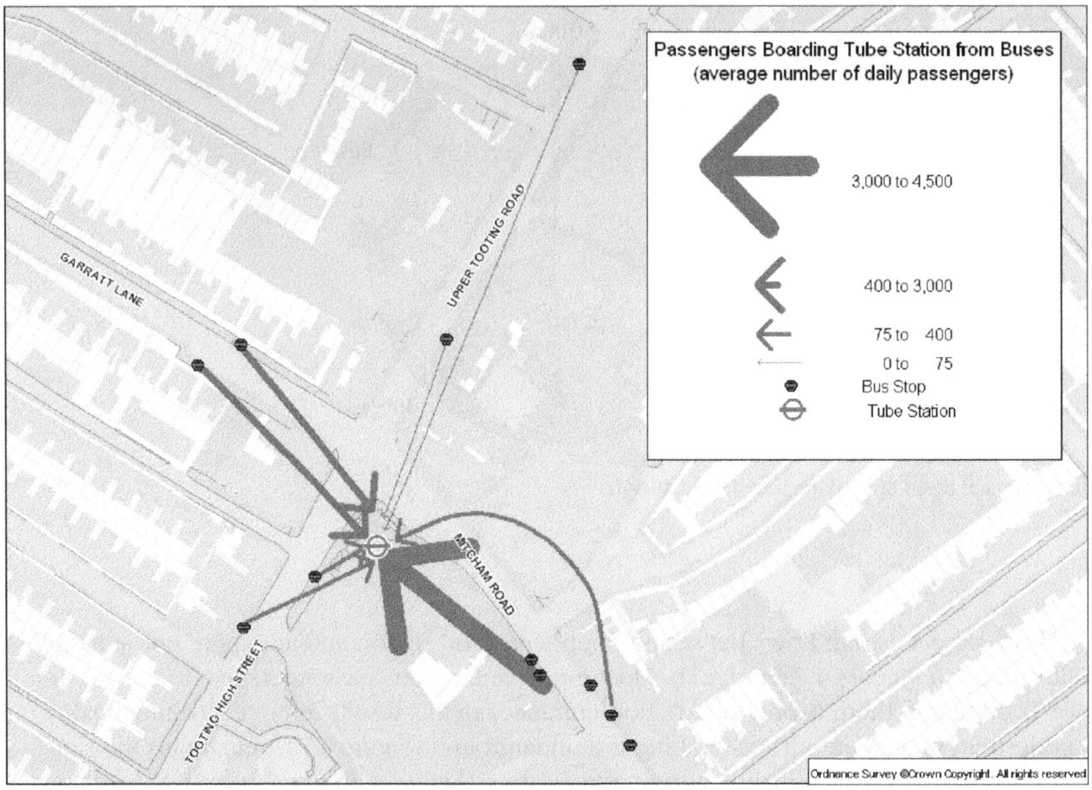

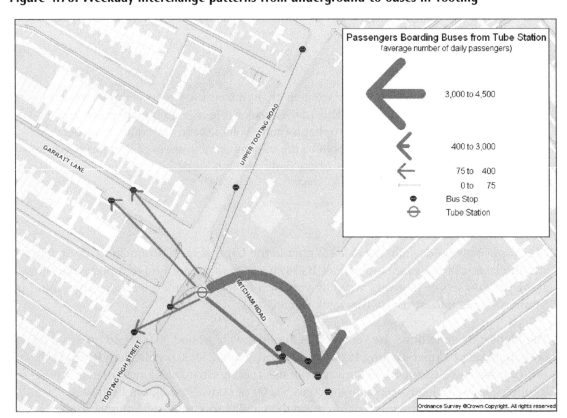

Source: TfL RODS and BODS data, average weekday.
Base: from underground to bus = 5,992; from bus to underground = 5,553.

Figure 4.7b: Weekday interchange patterns from underground to buses in Tooting

Source: TfL RODS and BODS data, average weekday.
Base: from underground to bus = 5,992; from bus to underground = 5,553.

Figure 4.8: Total number of pedestrians along sections of high street in Tooting and Ball Hill, between 08.00 and 19.00, on different days of the week

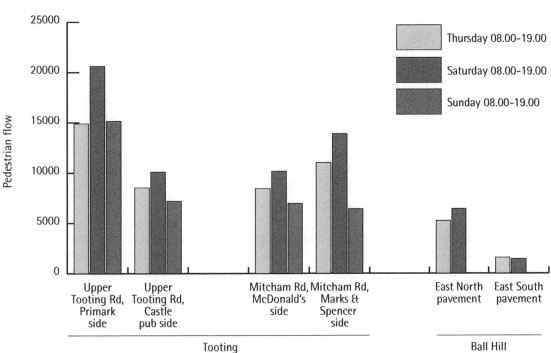

Source: CCTV analysis.

Pedestrians crossing the street

One of the characteristics of mixed-use streets is the high level of pedestrian crossing activity resulting, for example, from people visiting shops on opposite sides of the street, or boarding a bus across the street. Much of this activity occurs away from formal crossing points, and so is difficult to capture in surveys.

The highest volume of pedestrians at a formal crossing was found on the southern arm of Tooting Broadway junction, in the vicinity of the underground station, where crossing facilities are provided at the signalised junction. Around lunchtime, two-way flows reach 1,200 pedestrians per hour on a weekday, 1,100 per hour on a Sunday and the highest rate of 1,500 pedestrians per hour on a Saturday. Over the busiest 24-hour period, around 15,000 people use this formal crossing point – although substantial numbers also cross informally to the south, on a direct line of route between the underground station and the southbound bus stops (Figure 4.7b).

Streets as places for social interaction

The literature review in Chapter 1 referred to the Urban Task Force report (DETR, 1999), which argued that mixed-use streets could act as a 'social glue' that would bind members of a disparate neighbourhood together. There was some support for this notion in the focus groups, where local people reported being quite likely to come across 3their friends as they did their local shopping, and to often chatting informally with other people (for example, while waiting for a bus).

Pedestrians' activities on the street

Previous studies have concentrated on the needs of pedestrians as link users, or 'striders', using the street simply as a means of getting from A to B. From CCTV analysis, this study identified 10 distinct types of activities that pedestrians engage in while using mixed-use street as places, many of which are not recognised in current street design standards.

Browsers Browsers have an interest in what that particular mixed-use street has to offer, commercially and culturally: they are the 'window shoppers', and the tourists or visitors admiring the street scene as they walk along.

Socialisers Socialisers are there to meet others, to be seen and to converse with others. They tend to stand in groups or walk slowly along the footway, taking up considerable width and may often be oblivious to the needs of other footway users.

Observers These are usually more solitary people, who in the main observe other people on the street and their activities. They may be seated on a bench, enjoying outdoor facilities offered by a café or public house, or leaning against a wall.

Waiters These people arrange to meet others at an agreed landmark location along the street; others wait around on the street for friends to complete other tasks, such as shopping or visiting public toilets.

Resters These people sit down in order to rest and recuperate. They include disproportionate numbers of older people, and those with young children or with heavy shopping bags.

Queuers Many people queue on the street, to use a cash machine or a telephone, to wait for a shop to open, to gain entry to a club, or to buy something from a street vendor. They may also be queuing for a bus or taxi, or waiting to cross the road.

Workers From fruit and vegetables to seafood, street stalls are part of a vibrant mixed-use environment. Some stalls operate seasonally (for example, ice-cream sellers) or at night (hot-dog vendors). In addition, there are other people giving out leaflets, wearing sandwich boards, soliciting contributions for charities, or just begging. There are also various illegal street activities, such as soliciting for prostitution, or selling black market DVDs/CDs and cigarettes.

Entertainers The larger streets and associated public spaces attract street entertainers, ranging from musicians to jugglers and mime artists.

Customers Street workers and entertainers depend on customers. Transport also has its street customers, such as those buying bus tickets or feeding parking meters.

Inhabiters Finally, there are some people who are forced to reside on the street for lack of anywhere else to go during the day, or live at night. They may be living in bed-and-breakfast accommodation, or have nowhere to live at all. Shop doorways are appropriated as makeshift beds at night, while street drinkers inhabit particular spaces during the day. Many of these groups and their activities are generally labelled as being 'antisocial'.

Some of these activities are illustrated in the photographs opposite.

Browsers

Socialisers

Waiters

Mix of street activities

Queuers

Observers

Customers

Workers

This was explored more formally in the residents' surveys in the three case study areas, as shown in Figure 4.9. Here it was found that respondents were more likely to bump into people they knew while out shopping the longer they had lived in the area. The proportions seeing friends on the mixed-use street were highest in each length-of-residence group in Ball Hill, and generally lowest in Tooting, suggesting that the smaller shopping centres are better at fostering informal and unplanned social interaction.

Figure 4.9: Proportion of residents agreeing with the statement, 'I usually bump into people I know when out in the shopping area', by length of residence in area

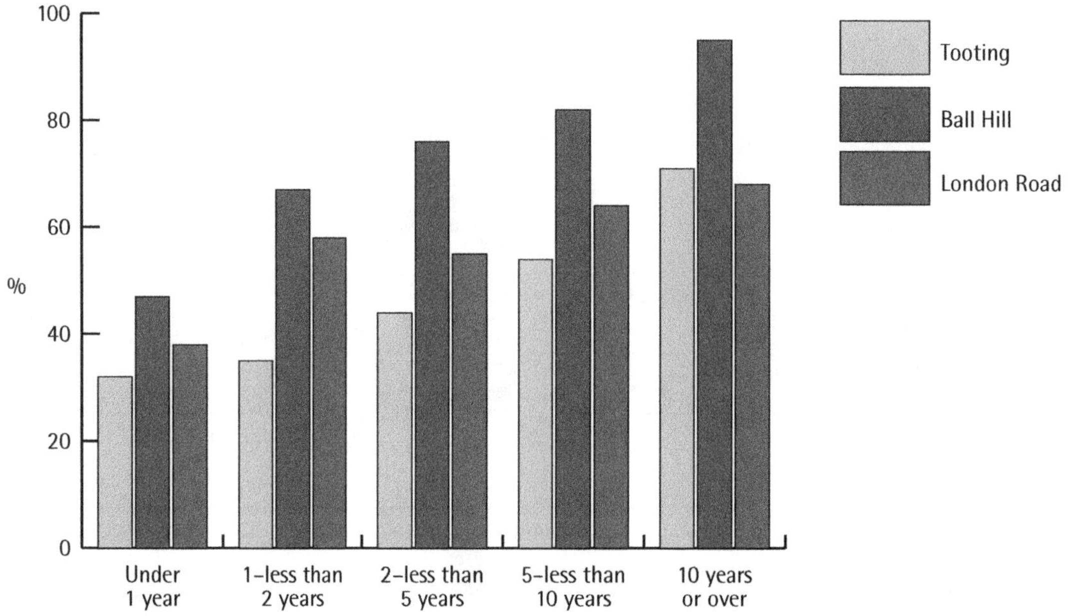

Source: Tooting and London Road residents' surveys, Ball Hill street-user survey (residents only).
Base: Tooting = 309, Ball Hill = 170, London Road = 207.

The opportunity to socialise with a friend or neighbour, encountered by chance on the street, is also facilitated by the provision of public amenities and the general attractiveness of the mixed-use street environment. CCTV observation in Tooting, for example, provides evidence for the social usefulness of such basic facilities as public seating, as illustrated in Figure 4.10.

Role of street amenities: a day in the life of a bench

Public amenities can act as an important focus for street activities, both during the day and at night. While in some contexts, certain types of activity can appear threatening, for example when they are appropriated 'antisocially' by young or drunk people, in many situations street amenities enrich public space and act as a catalyst for a range of social street life.

Using CCTV footage, Figure 4.10 illustrates how two adjacent benches on Upper Tooting Road add to the richness of the street environment and facilitate some of the different kinds of informal street activity illustrated on page 51. People are seen at all times of day and night congregating around them; using them as a resting point, somewhere to wait for the shops to open, a place to stop and talk with friends, or to watch the world go by.

Figure 4.10: Illustration of activities through the day and night, centred around two benches on Upper Tooting Road

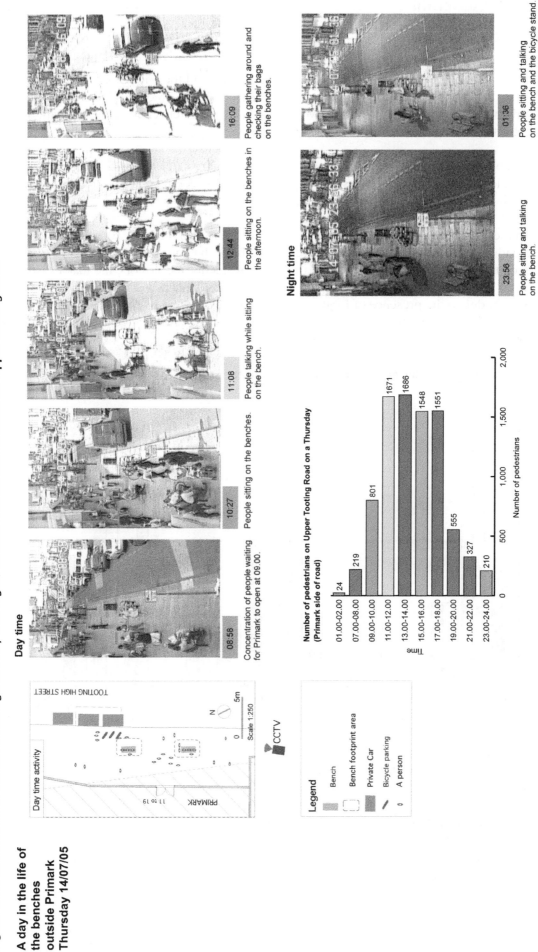

Street-user profiles

Who visits mixed-use streets?

Street users are drawn both from the local community and the wider area. In the latter case, this partly reflects the important role of the mixed-use street as a link within the urban road and public transport networks, but is mainly a reflection of the reputation and attractiveness of the place and its local businesses.

Taking age and ethnicity as indicators of diversity, Figures 4.11 and 4.12 compare the profiles of residents and visitors intercepted in the on-street interviews in the three case study areas. They show both interesting differences and similarities.

In the case of **age groups**, around half the adult street users in both Tooting and London Road are in the 25-44 age group, whereas in Ball Hill the age profile is much more even (see Figure 4.11). Comparing the age profiles of residents and visitors, the major disparity is on London Road, where there are twice as many residents as visitors in the 16-24 age group, due to the presence of local student residences; it appears to be the older age groups from outside the local area that are disproportionately attracted by the services on offer here.

Figure 4.11: Age profiles of residents and visitors to the study areas

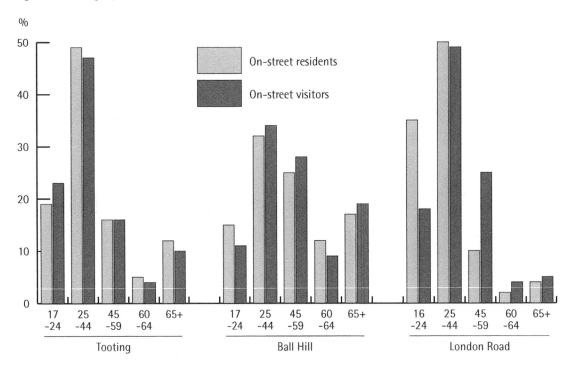

Source: street-user surveys.
Base: Tooting = 512, Ball Hill = 489, London Road = 405.

Patterns of **ethnicity** also differ across the three study areas, and between local residents and visitors. Tooting is clearly the most ethnically diverse of the three sites, as was acknowledged in the residents' focus groups. When asked how they would describe Tooting to a person who did not know the area, the typical response was:

> 'First thing I'd say is multicultural. We've got every kind of person living here. Got a big Black community, big Asian community I think recently there's been a lot of Chinese. It's very multicultural.' (Older resident, female)

This is confirmed in Figure 4.12, which shows that only around a half of the street users interviewed in Tooting were White, compared with around 80% in the other two areas. Furthermore, Tooting attracts a higher proportion of non-White visitors than are found among the resident population, whereas in the other areas more of the visitors are White than are the residents, particularly on London Road. Although many of the establishments on London Road offer Asian food, it is interesting to note that fewer of the visitors than local residents are Asian or Chinese.

Figure 4.12: Ethnicity profiles of residents and visitors to the study areas

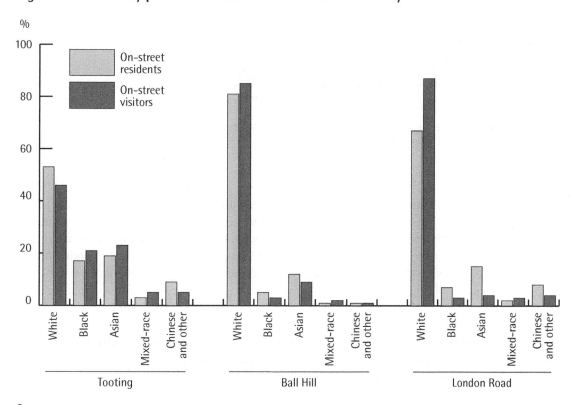

Source: street-user surveys.
Base: Tooting = 512, Ball Hill = 489, London Road = 405.

How well are mobility-restricted groups represented?

In both the resident and on-street surveys, respondents were asked whether they experienced a range of disabilities, including learning, hearing, visual and physical mobility restrictions. By far the most commonly reported was some form of physical mobility disability. Figure 4.13 shows the proportion of respondents indicating that they have a mobility disability. Note that in Ball Hill there was no separate household-based survey of residents.

The sample sizes are very small, so care is needed in drawing firm conclusions, but at face value the three areas show large differences in the proportion of respondents with mobility difficulties. The proportion is lowest in Tooting and highest in Ball Hill, and differs by a factor of three. This could partly – though not fully – be explained by differences in levels of social deprivation and the varying age distributions of residents and visitors, with older people more common around the Ball Hill area.

Figure 4.13: Percentage of respondents reporting a mobility disability

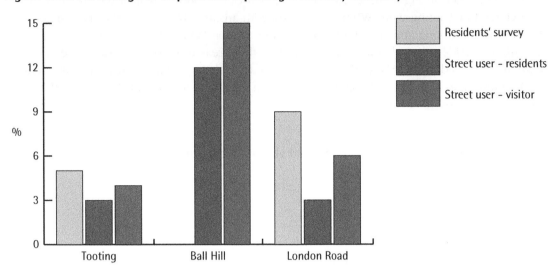

Source: residents' survey, street-user surveys (residents), street-user surveys (visitors).
Base: Tooting = 14/5/15, Ball Hill = 21/48, London Road = 18/7/9.

According to the on-street surveys, there are higher proportions of mobility-impaired people among the visitors than the residents in all three areas, suggesting that the streets are relatively attractive to people with such restrictions. On the other hand, in the two areas where comparable household-based resident surveys were carried out (Tooting and London Road), it seems that mobility-restricted residents are under-represented on the mixed-use streets, although this may be due to the different sampling methods that were used.[3]

From video analysis of the two streets in Tooting and of two sections of Walsgrave Road in Ball Hill, a count was taken of the numbers of wheelchairs, mobility vehicles and pushchairs or buggies observed. The results are summarised in Table 4.1.

Table 4.1: Total pushchair and wheelchair numbers in Tooting and Ball Hill

	Tooting		Ball Hill	
	Upper Tooting Road	**Mitcham Road**	**Central section**	**Eastern section**
Thursday 08.00–19.00 (pushchairs)	3% (698)	2% (446)	2% (158)	4% (248)
Saturday 08.00–19.00 (pushchairs)	2% (640)	2% (434)	2% (187)	3% (269)
Sunday 08.00–19.00 (pushchairs)	2% (530)	2% (303)	N/A	N/A
Thursday 08.00–19.00 (wheelchairs)	<1% (14)	<1% (22)	0% (0)	<1% (4)
Saturday 08.00–19.00 (wheelchairs)	<1% (18)	<1% (22)	<1% (12)	<1% (10)
Sunday 08.00–19.00 (wheelchairs)	<1% (14)	<1% (22)	N/A	N/A

Source: CCTV analysis.

---

[3]   The on-street survey provides a sample of visits to the street, while the resident survey is a sample of those living in the area. So, if residents with mobility restrictions make, on average, fewer trips per week to their local high street than other groups of residents, then they will be under-represented in the on-street surveys.

Pushchair use is largely constant across both areas at around 2% of the total observed pedestrian flow. The census states that the percentage of the population under five is 6% for Tooting and 7% for Ball Hill, so this might suggest that young children are under-represented on these streets, although this is likely to reflect their generally home-centred activity patterns, rather than any deterrent effect of using these streets per se.

Across both sites the proportion of wheelchair users is minimal. However, there is no available data on the extent of wheelchair use in general against which to benchmark these findings. There remains a concern, however, that many wheelchair uses may be deterred from using the case study streets.

Why do people visit mixed-use streets?

Mixed-use streets are traditionally associated with being important retail centres, but most offer a much wider range of services, and have adapted to the growing demand for an increase in eating and drinking activities.

The reasons given in the on-street surveys for visiting the three case study streets show certain similarities and differences between the resident and visitor populations, as shown in Figure 4.14. In particular:

* shopping is the most commonly stated reason for residents visiting each case study street, but in the case of London Road visitors are more likely to come to the area to eat or drink than to shop;
* in Ball Hill, shopping is the main attraction for over two thirds of both residents and visitor street users – a much higher proportion than in the other two areas;
* between 11% and 15% of non-resident street users are visiting friends and relatives in the area;
* between 10% and 25% of street users are carrying out other activities in the area;
* work/study activities generally account for less than 10% of the reasons for visiting the areas; and
* in all cases, leisure activities are the most commonly stated reason for visiting a mixed-use street for less than 10% of respondents.

Figure 4.14a: Reasons why residents visit the case study streets

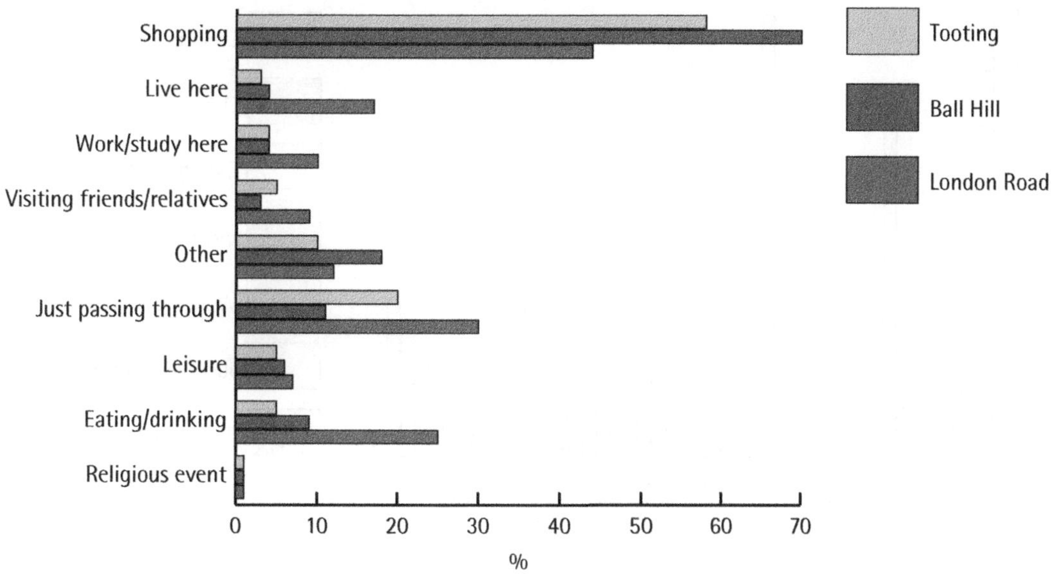

Source: street-user surveys.
Base: Tooting = 512, Ball Hill = 489, London Road = 405.

Figure 4.14b: Reasons why visitors visit the case study streets

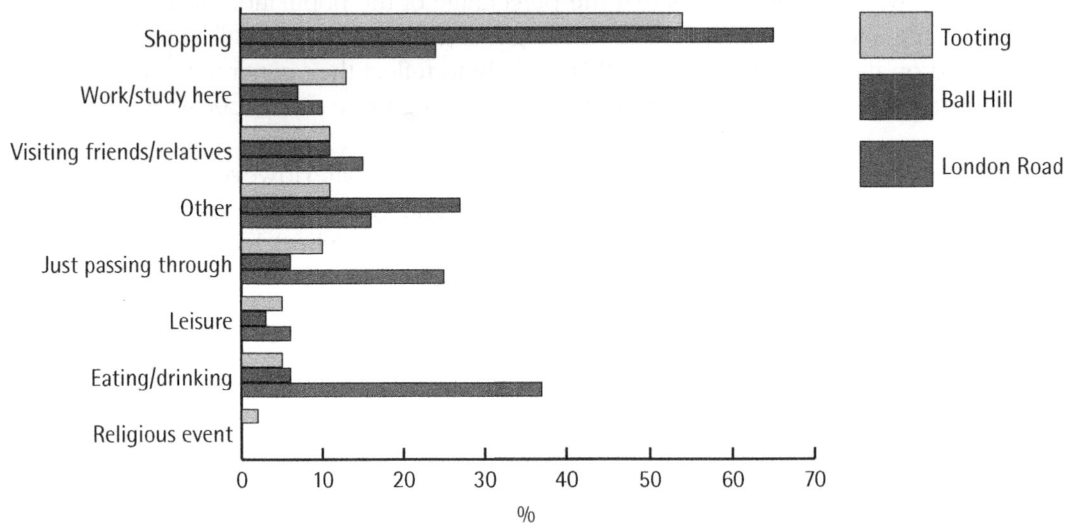

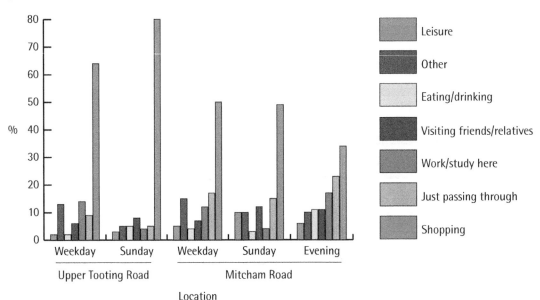

Source: street-user surveys.
Base: Tooting = 512, Ball Hill = 489, London Road = 405.

How do reasons for visiting vary by location and time period?

With the introduction of Sunday trading, some mixed-use streets now function as major retail centres seven days a week, and may offer some services 24 hours a day. However, their character can vary markedly by location along the street and time of day.

The kinds of people visiting mixed-use streets, and the reasons they are there, differ by day of week and time of day, and according to the services on offer at different times and locations in the area. This variety is illustrated using data from the Tooting case study.

The mix of reasons for visiting the street is heavily influenced by the location of services and their opening times, as shown in Figure 4.15.

Figure 4.15: Reasons for visiting Tooting, by location and time period

Source: Tooting street-user survey, total sample of 512 respondents.

Note that:

- Upper Tooting Road has a higher proportion of people who are shopping, both on weekdays and on Sundays than Mitcham Road.
- The peak shopping day on Upper Tooting Road is a Sunday, with 80% of street users shopping (64% on a weekday), compared with 50% on a Sunday on Mitcham Road.
- Mitcham Road has a very similar user profile on a weekday and a Sunday.
- Mitcham Road has a higher proportion of people 'just passing through' (particularly on a weekday evening), which reflects the major interchange flows between the underground station and the bus stops on both sides of the road, as well as people walking home from the station.

The differences in activities by location and time period are associated with different street-user profiles.

Looking first at **age groups**, Figure 4.16 shows, in particular, that:

- the older age groups (above 55) form a much higher proportion of street users on weekdays than on a Sunday;
- Mitcham Road appeals to a much older age group, particularly on a weekday; and
- by early evening on Mitcham Road, there are few older people, and the profile more closely matches that of a Sunday.

Figure 4.16: Age profiles in Tooting, by location and time period

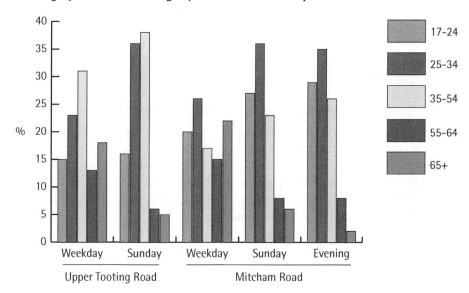

Source: Tooting street-user survey, total sample of 512 respondents.

The **ethnicity profiles** also show interesting differences by location and time period (Figure 4.17). Here we see that:

- on a weekday, Upper Tooting Road is much more commonly used by non-White groups (60% of street users), compared with Mitcham Road (40% non-White);
- on a Sunday, there are no significant differences between the two roads, although there are marginally more non-White users on Mitcham Road; and
- by early evening, the profile of users on Mitcham Road again more closely matches that on a Sunday.

Figure 4.17: Ethnicity profiles in Tooting, by location and time period

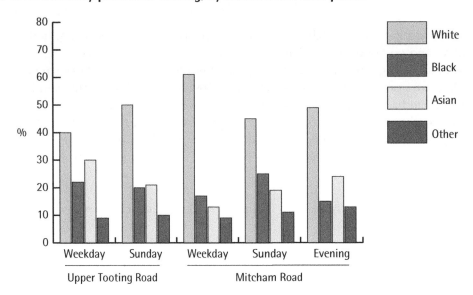

Source: Tooting street-user survey, total sample of 512 respondents.

The changing patterns of use over the day of a mixed-use street can also be observed from an analysis of the CCTV data. The example opposite (Figure 4.18) illustrates how the overall pattern of use of a section of street on Mitcham Road changes over a 24-hour period on a Saturday. This clearly shows differences in the overall intensity of street use, by day and night, for both vehicles and pedestrians, and the changing balance of activity between the two sides of the street, as daytime shopping activity gives way to night-time drinking and eating activities.

Note, in particular, the following, as shown in the photographs:

- 05.41: there is some early morning loading activity, before the street becomes busy;
- 08.50: the area is relatively quiet, due to the lack of commuting to work on a Saturday, with light road traffic and pedestrian activity on both sides of the street;
- 12.15 and 15.59: the street is full of traffic and pedestrian activity, with more of the latter on the east side, alongside the main multiple stores;
- 21.44, 22.53 and 00.47: activity switches to the west side of the street, both in terms of pedestrian activity and parked cars, where the bars and clubs are located; and
- 02.10: traffic activity dies down, although some pedestrians can still be seen congregating on the west side of the street where night-time activities take place.

How do people travel to the area?

Figure 4.19 compares the methods of transport that were used by residents and visitors to reach the mixed-use streets, as reported in the on-street interviews in Tooting, Ball Hill and London Road. In all three cases, 80-90% of residents had reached the area on foot, and this did not seem to depend on proximity to the street. Visitors used a much wider range of modes of transport, with private car being used by over 40% of visitors to Ball Hill and London Road, but only 20% in Tooting, where there was a correspondingly higher level of public transport use (over 40% by bus and 15% by underground). Bus use among visitors was lowest on London Road (11%).

Figure 4.18: Activities on Mitcham Road over a 24-hour period

Saturday 18/06/05

Daytime

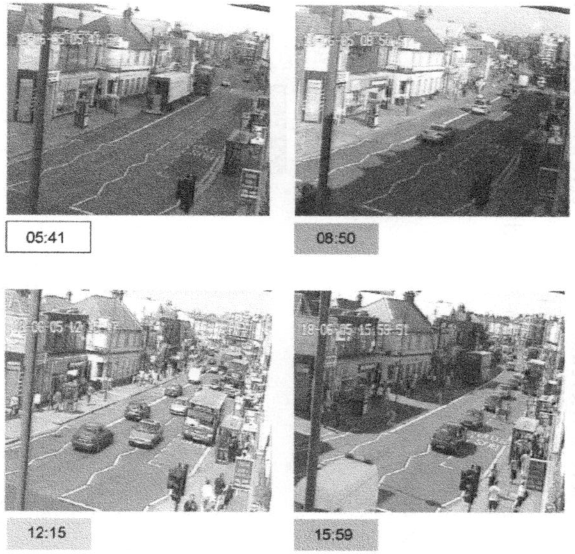

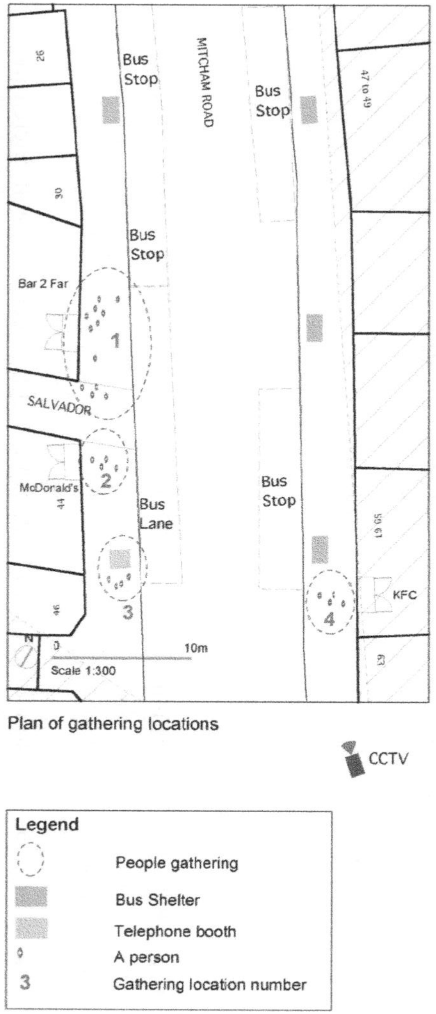

05:41

08:50

12:15

15:59

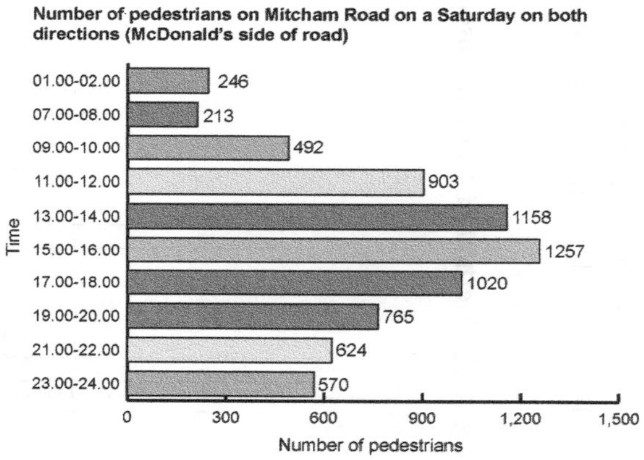

Night-time

21:44

22:53

00:47

02:10

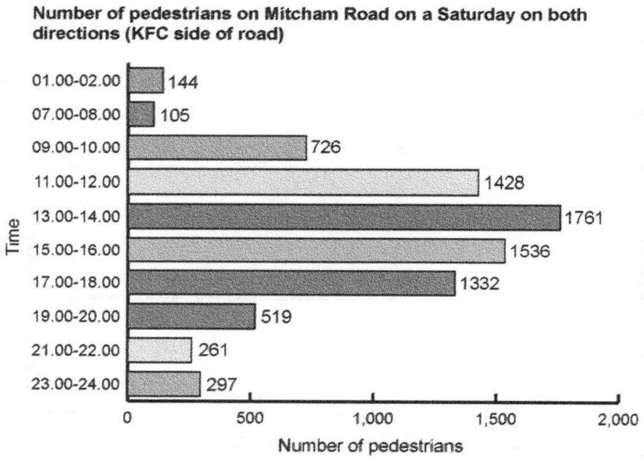

MITCHAM ROAD

47 to 49

59 61

63

KFC

Bus Stop

Bus Stop

Bus Stop

Bus Stop

Bus Lane

26

30

Bar 2 Far

SALVADOR

McDonald's

44

46

1

2

3

4

CCTV

Scale 1:300

10m

N

Plan of gathering locations

Legend

People gathering

Bus Shelter

Telephone booth

A person

3 — Gathering location number

Number of pedestrians on Mitcham Road on a Saturday on both directions (KFC side of road)

Time	Number of pedestrians
01.00–02.00	144
07.00–08.00	105
09.00–10.00	726
11.00–12.00	1428
13.00–14.00	1761
15.00–16.00	1536
17.00–18.00	1332
19.00–20.00	519
21.00–22.00	261
23.00–24.00	297

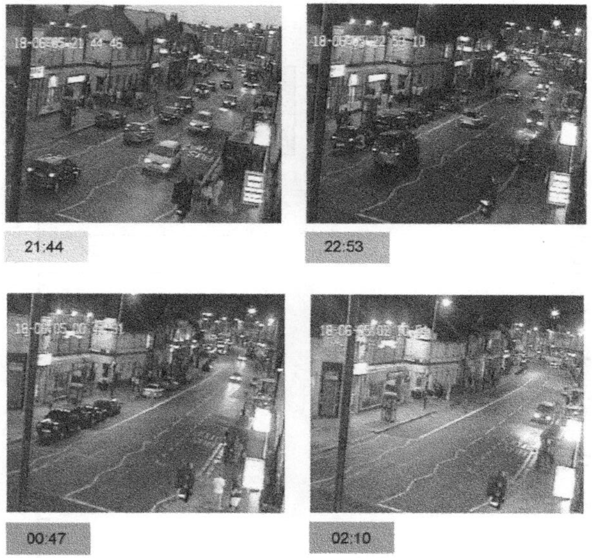

Number of pedestrians on Mitcham Road on a Saturday on both directions (McDonald's side of road)

Time	Number of pedestrians
01.00–02.00	246
07.00–08.00	213
09.00–10.00	492
11.00–12.00	903
13.00–14.00	1158
15.00–16.00	1257
17.00–18.00	1020
19.00–20.00	765
21.00–22.00	624
23.00–24.00	570

Figure 4.19: Method of transport used to access the mixed-use streets

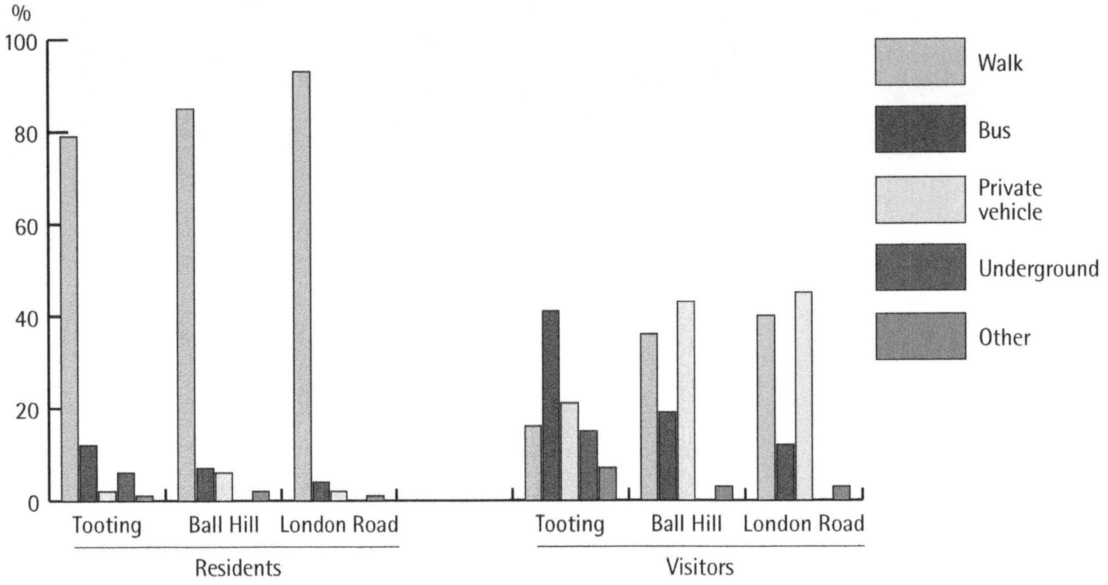

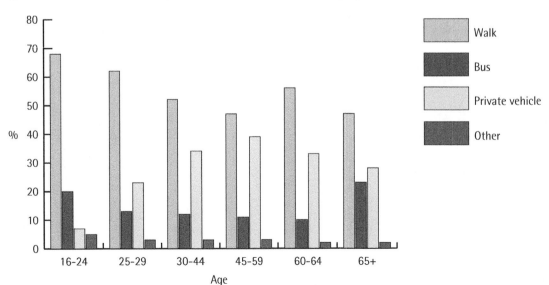

Source: street-user surveys
Base: Tooting = 177/335, Ball Hill = 170/319, London Road = 242/163.

Influence of age and travel frequency

Using Ball Hill as an example (which is broadly replicated in the other two areas), there are clear differences in the likelihood of respondents travelling to the street on foot, both among residents and visitors, according to their age group and frequency of travel.

The percentage of respondents who walk to the centre decreases with increasing age, until the age group 60-64 (Figure 4.20), where it increases. Conversely, the percentage of respondents using a private vehicle to reach Ball Hill increases with age, up until ages 45-59. Bus use is U-shaped, being at its highest among the 16-24 and 65+ age groups.

Figure 4.20: Method of transport used to access Ball Hill, by age

Source: Ball Hill street-user survey.
Base = 489.

The majority of those who visit Ball Hill every day come on foot (Figure 4.21), and this percentage drops consistently with decreasing frequency of visit, from 80% for daily visitors down to 15% of those visiting less than once a month. Conversely, the percentage of those who use a private vehicle to access the area increases with decreasing frequency of visit, from a low of 5% to a high of 65%. There is no clear trend among bus users.

Figure 4.21: Method of transport used to access Ball Hill, by frequency of visit

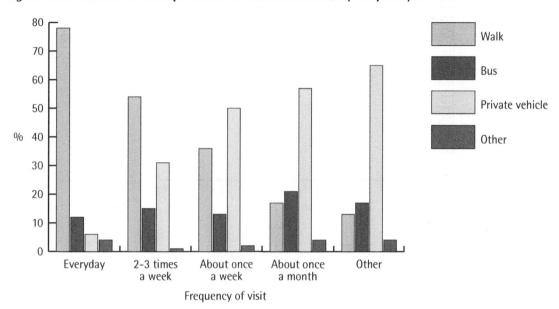

Source: Ball Hill street-user survey.
Base = 489.

Methods of access to the streets also varied with other characteristics of the street users. In Tooting, for example, differences were found according to the ethnic group of respondents. White users were most likely to walk and Black respondents least so. Conversely, Black users were most likely to arrive by bus, and White users least so; Asian users were equally likely to use both modes. Black users were more likely to arrive by car than the other groups.

Customer profiles

Where do business customers come from?

Historically, the larger mixed-use streets have grown up at key points on the urban road network, where businesses have been able to access a larger customer base than can be provided by the local community. The on-street surveys corroborated this, finding that street users include large numbers of visitors to the area in addition to the local residents.

In the business survey, respondents were asked from where they drew their customer base; the results are summarised in Figure 4.22. While there is some evidence that the larger the centre, the broader the catchment area, this relationship is not as strong as might have been expected.

Virtually all the businesses interviewed drew some of their customers from their local residential population. In Tooting, all businesses attracted some of customers from the surrounding areas as well, while in the other centres only around 80% did so. Interestingly, in each area about one third of businesses reported having a regional catchment.

In Tooting, the largest of the three sites, around 10% of businesses reported having customers from abroad.

Figure 4.22: Business-reported customer catchment areas, by case study area

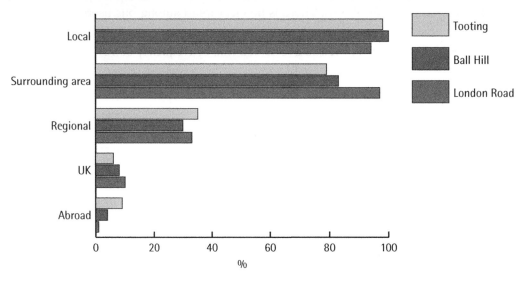

Source: business surveys.
Base: Tooting = 150, Ball Hill = 78, London Road = 87.

Do businesses' customer profiles reflect the local area in general?

The business survey asked respondents to describe their customer profile, in terms of age group, gender, ethnicity and religion. They could either report that they reflected the area in general, or indicate how their customers' profile differed. Figure 4.23 shows the proportion of businesses in each area reporting that their customer base reflected that area in general, on three of the criteria[4] (excluding gender). In the case of ethnicity and religion, in all three areas responses ranged between 75% and 90%. However, in the case of age group, less than half of the businesses in Tooting perceived themselves to have customers who reflected the age profile of the local area as a whole.

Figure 4.23: Proportion of businesses stating that their customers reflected the area in general, on three sociodemographic criteria

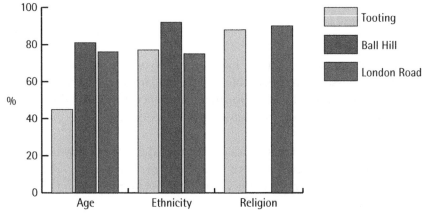

Source: business surveys.
Base: Tooting = 150, Ball Hill = 78, London Road = 87.

---

[4]   The question concerning religion was not asked in Ball Hill, at the request of the local authority.

A further analysis was carried out on those businesses in Tooting that reported an atypical customer base. Over 90% of businesses that did not consider their customers to reflect the area in general stated that their customers were aged between 25 and 44. Tooting is a large district centre and as such it provides more specialist shops than the other two areas, particularly clothing stores. Typically, these stores seem to be aimed at this economically active age group.

How long do customers spend in the area?

Respondents interviewed on-street were asked how long they intended to stay in the vicinity of the mixed-use street during that visit. Figure 4.24 shows the average responses for residents and visitors, but only for people who said that they were shopping or carrying out some other commercial activity in the area.[5]

Figure 4.24: Time spent in the area per visit by street users shopping or carrying out another commercial activity

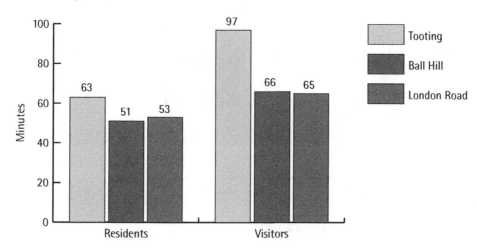

Source: street-user surveys.
Base: Tooting = 309, Ball Hill = 391, London Road = 249.

This shows that, in all three areas, visitors spend longer, on average, in the centre than residents, and that durations are greater in the larger centre of Tooting than elsewhere, particularly for visitors. In Ball Hill and on London Road, visitors on average stay in the area about 15 minutes longer than residents, but for Tooting the difference is more than 30 minutes.

The distributions of time spent on London Road show interesting differences between the daytime and evening street users. While around half of those interviewed reported spending less than 30 minutes in the area in both time periods, there was a significant secondary peak in the evening in the one to two hours range (around 30% of respondents), probably reflecting a significant number of people who are attracted to the area to eat and drink at night.

---

[5] The questionnaires asked for an estimate of time in the area in duration bands, so the average values shown here have simply used the midpoints from each time band.

How much money do customers spend in the area?

We first examine financial expenditure in terms of averages per trip, and then look at the effects of differences in trip frequency by method of transport on total expenditure over a period of time.

Average expenditure

Figure 4.25 shows the average reported expenditure per visit for residents and visitors, across the three areas.[6] Both roughly mirror the distributions of average time spent in the area, with some exceptions.

Figure 4.25: Average expenditure per visit in each area by residents and visitors shopping or carrying out another commercial activity

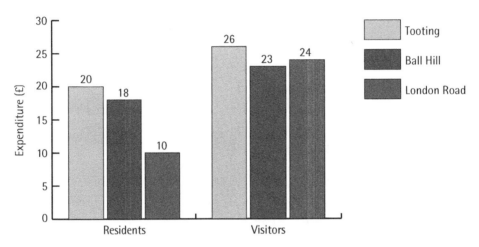

Source: street-user surveys.
Base: Tooting = 309, Ball Hill = 391, London Road = 249.

Average visitor spend per trip is higher than for the local residents in all three areas. Rather surprisingly, average visitor spend is very similar across the three areas, with Tooting only being slightly higher than the others, even though people reported spending substantially longer per visit in that area than in Ball Hill or London Road – perhaps reflecting the greater opportunities for comparison shopping in the larger centre. For residents, however, there are much greater differences, with the average reported spend per trip on London Road being around half that of Tooting and Ball Hill – probably reflecting the need for local residents to look elsewhere for most of their daily requirements (as observed in Figure 4.14).

Effects of frequency of visit and mode of transport

Figure 4.26 demonstrates that the less often a person visits the street, the more they spend per visit. This is the case in all three areas, with the differences being the least on London Road (ranging from £18 for daily users to £22 for monthly users) and the greatest in Ball Hill (from £9 daily, up to an average of £27 for monthly visitors).

---

[6] The questionnaires asked for an estimate of expenditure in the area in cost bands, so the average values shown here and later figures have simply used the midpoints from each band.

Figure 4.26: Average expenditure per visit, by frequency of visit (shopping or other commercial activity)

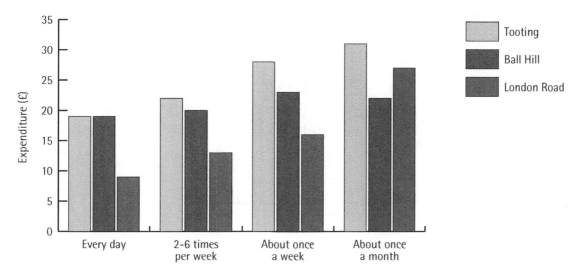

Source: street-user surveys.
Base: Tooting = 309, Ball Hill = 391, London Road = 249.

Customers travelling by car visit less often than those arriving on foot and spend between £5 and £10 more per trip, as can be seen in Figure 4.27. Bus-user expenditure lies between these two extremes. Only in Tooting is the average expenditure of bus users similar to that of car users; in Ball Hill, those arriving on foot have a similar average spend to those coming by bus, but not in the other two areas, where those on foot spend less.

Figure 4.27: Average expenditure per visit, by method of transport used to reach the street (shopping or other commercial activity)

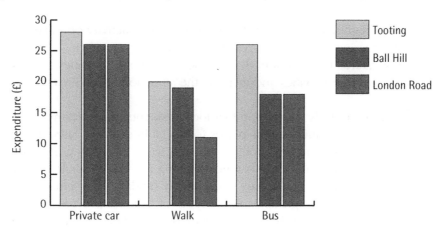

Source: street-user surveys.
Base: Tooting = 309, Ball Hill = 391, London Road = 249.

Figure 4.27 can give the impression that car-borne customers are the ones who spend the most on mixed-use streets. However, once differences in trip frequency are taken into account, and an estimate is made of average expenditure per customer per week, the pattern changes, as shown in Figure 4.28. Across the three areas, average expenditure by car-borne customers is slightly below that of bus users, with those arriving on foot having the highest weekly spend – although because of the variations between sites, differences are not statistically significant.

Figure 4.28: Average weekly expenditure, by method of transport used to reach the street (shopping or other commercial activities)

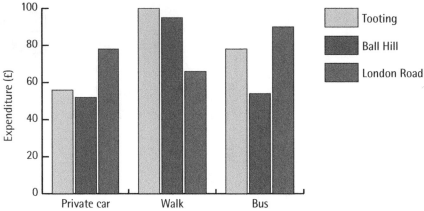

Source: street-user surveys.
Base: Tooting = 309, Ball Hill = 391, London Road = 249.

Summary

The busier of the mixed-use case study streets are very intensively used during the course of a day. The extreme example is provided by Tooting, where the main roads each accommodate approximately 15,000 to 20,000 vehicles per day, and the footways around 30,000 pedestrians per day. At the busy Tooting Broadway junction, around which are clustered the larger shops and the underground station, combined vehicle flows can exceed 30,000 vehicles per day through the junction, and pedestrian flows in the vicinity are around 50,000 people per day – resulting in an extremely intensive node of conflict and activity. When this activity is looked at in more detail, we find that, as well as being a major shopping centre, the streets of Tooting form an important transport interchange, not just between bus/walk and the underground, but more so between bus and bus.

The video analysis identified 10 different forms of pedestrian activity on mixed-use streets, apart from people passing through the area. Most of these occur informally and are not fully recognised or catered for in current design guidance. Public amenities, such as seating, can help to enhance street activities and increase the attraction of the area as a place.

The surveys in each case study area found that local residents make extensive use of their local high street, and value them as places for social interaction. Street-user profiles generally reflect local ethnic and age profiles – though some disability groups appear to be under-represented – while at the same time attracting a broad clientele from a much wider catchment area. Patterns of use vary considerably by day and evening, reflecting the lifestyles of different population groups and the types of facilities provided on the different streets. Overall, most customers arrive on foot or by other sustainable travel modes.

Customers who are visitors to the area generally spend more time and more money per visit than local residents. However, while on average visitors to Tooting reported spending more time there than visitors to Ball Hill or London Road, this was not matched by a correspondingly higher expenditure per trip. In general, people who visit mixed-use streets less often spend more money per visit than the more frequent street users, and frequency varies according to method of travel. As a consequence, while car users spend most per trip, those arriving on foot spend more over a period of time because they visit the mixed-use street more often.

In the next chapter, we examine how the provision of facilities on mixed-use streets and patterns of use are reflected in perceptions and attitudes towards these streets.

5

What do users think about mixed-use streets as places?

Findings from the user and business surveys

Residents' overall satisfaction with their streets

Residents were asked whether they liked their area, and enjoyed using the mixed-use streets. Figure 5.1 shows that, in all three areas, around 80% of residents agreed with the statement, 'I feel very comfortable living in the Tooting/Ball Hill/London Road area'. In Tooting, 78% further agreed that 'I enjoy using these [mixed-use] streets', while in London Road the agreement level rose to 87% (this question was not asked in Ball Hill). As one of the older women in the focus groups commented:

> 'My children love Tooting ... I love Tooting. Lots of my friends who have moved out still come back to shop in Tooting.'

Figure 5.1: Views of residents concerning their local area

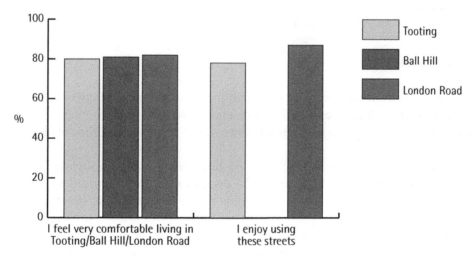

Source: street-user and residents' surveys.
Base: Tooting = 309, Ball Hill (on-street residents) = 170, London Road = 207.

However, when we look in more detail at different facets of conditions on mixed-use streets, a more complex and disturbing picture emerges.

Customer and business satisfaction with local businesses

Residents and visitors who were shopping or using other services along the mixed-use streets were asked a series of questions in the on-street survey about how satisfied they were with aspects of local business provision, in terms of the range and quality of provision, and the friendliness of the staff. The questions and responses are summarised in Figure 5.2.

Figure 5.2: Customer satisfaction with local businesses (percentage very/fairly satisfied)

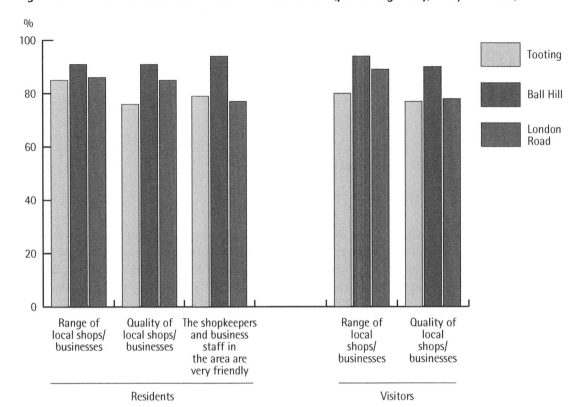

Source: Street-user surveys
Base: Tooting = 309, Ball Hill = 391, London Road = 249.

Overall we find that:

- Levels of satisfaction are generally very high in all three areas, at between 75% and 95%, with resident and visitor views in the same area being very similar.
- On all counts, the most satisfied respondents were the ones using the smallest centre, Ball Hill.
- Surprisingly, given the range of facilities, Tooting generally scored slightly lower on all three questions, and below London Road – even though the local residents in that area reported that most of their daily requirements were not met on that street.

The Tooting focus groups confirmed people's general satisfaction with the variety and vibrancy of what is on offer in the area, although the provision of furniture stores and some electrical goods was felt to be limited. In addition, some young people identified one deficiency in local provision:

'What I think Tooting is really missing is a night scene. It needs to have like better clubs, or whatever.' (Younger resident, male)

Among businesses, satisfaction with local trading conditions was also reasonably high overall (Figure 5.3). Around 90% of businesses in Ball Hill agreed with the statement that 'Tooting/Ball Hill/London Road is a good place to run a business like mine', compared with just over 70% of businesses in the other two areas. This is in agreement with the higher satisfaction ratings for Ball Hill in the street-user surveys.

Figure 5.3: Businesses' responses to the statement, 'Tooting/Ball Hill/London Road is a good place to run a business like mine'

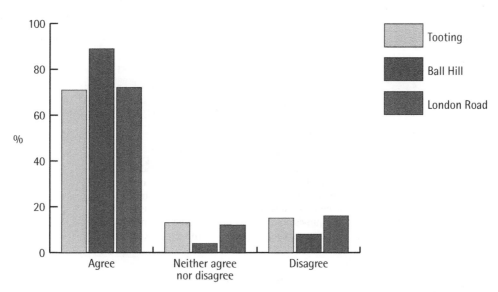

Source: business survey questionnaire.
Base: Tooting = 150, Ball Hill = 78, London Road = 87.

Tooting has the busiest streets of the three areas (Chapter 4), and local residents felt that they had become more so over time:

'I would say it's got more populated over the years. It's busier during the daytime and early evenings the streets are really packed.' (Younger resident, female)

'And Saturday afternoons on Tooting high street are really packed.' (Younger resident, male)

Both comments, however, were made in a positive way, indicating that the place had more of a buzz about it nowadays.

Satisfaction with access to the area

Street users were asked for their views about access to the high street where they were interviewed, both by bus and in relation to levels of car-parking provision. Responses are shown in Figure 5.4, as levels of *dis*satisfaction with bus services and parking provision; the latter is compared with the views of local businesses.

As can be seen, there is very little customer dissatisfaction with bus provision in any of the areas, with only between 4% and 6% of respondents identifying this as a concern; clearly, the case study mixed-use streets are perceived to be very accessible by bus. The proportions expressing dissatisfaction with car parking are greater, at between 37% and 40%. Although much higher, this is still a minority concern and contrasts strongly with the perception of businesses, where on average double this proportion feel that their customers have problems with car parking, with figures ranging from 71% to 86% of businesses expressing dissatisfaction.

This greater concern about customer car-parking provision among businesses probably reflects the greater spend per trip by car-borne customers, as noted in Figure 4.27, and a common perception among businesses that higher proportions of their customers arrive by car than is actually the case. It may also be that businesses feel that their car-borne

Figure 5.4: Dissatisfaction with access to the areas by bus and car

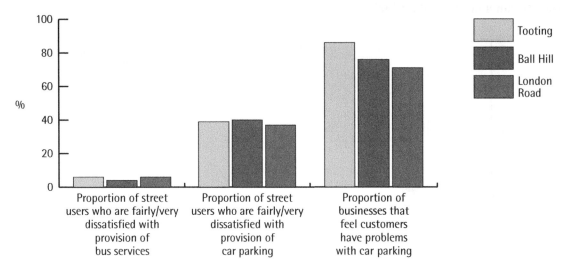

Source: Street-user and business surveys.
Base: Tooting = 512/150, Ball Hill = 489/78, London Road = 405/87.

customers have access to a larger number of alternative destinations than users of other transport modes, and so are less captive.

Concerns about the lack of provision of public amenities

In the street-user surveys, residents and visitors were asked about their degree of dissatisfaction with the availability of a series of public amenities that are commonly provided on busier and better-quality mixed-use streets (Figure 5.5).

Figure 5.5: Dissatisfaction with local amenities (percentage very/fairly dissatisfied)

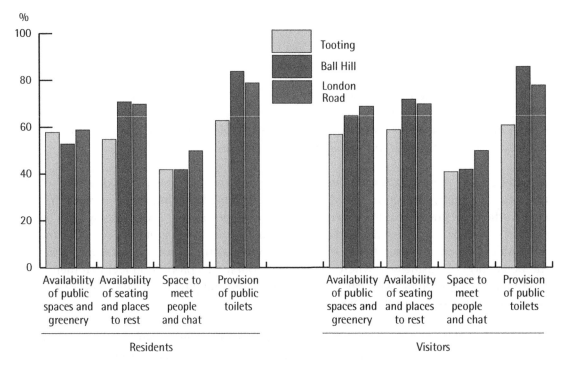

Source: street-user surveys (residents and visitors).
Base: Tooting = 177/335, Ball Hill = 170/319, London Road = 242/163.

Generally, dissatisfaction levels on the three case-study streets were high. Across all three areas, the amenity that users were overwhelmingly dissatisfied with was the provision of public toilets. Dissatisfaction ranged from 62% of those surveyed in Tooting to 85% in Ball Hill. 'Availability of seating and places to rest', and 'availability of public spaces and greenery' both had dissatisfaction scores of between 55% and 70%, with generally lower satisfaction levels in Tooting than in the other two areas. The only amenity with a negative score not exceeding 50% was 'space to meet people and chat'. Scores were very similar for residents and visitors to the area.

Levels of dissatisfaction with the provision of public toilets among businesses were slightly higher than the public levels shown in Figure 5.5, ranging from 70% in Tooting to 87% on London Road and 88% in Ball Hill.

Concerns over poor levels of cleanliness

Dissatisfaction with the lack of cleanliness on mixed-use streets appears to be fairly high among street users (Figure 5.6). In total, 57% of Tooting street-users, 51% of Ball Hill street-users and 46% of London Road street-users stated that they were fairly or very dissatisfied with the cleanliness of the area. Residents were generally less satisfied with conditions in their area than visitors. Businesses also appeared to be fairly unhappy, but Tooting businesses were much less likely to be dissatisfied compared with their counterparts in the other two case study areas.

Figure 5.6: Dissatisfaction with the amounts of litter and graffiti (percentage very/fairly dissatisfied)

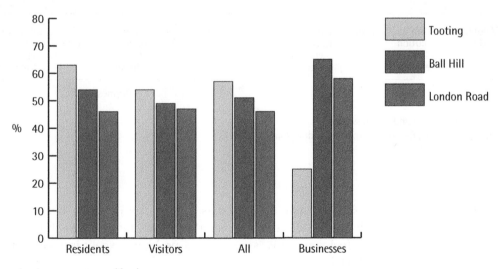

Source: street-user survey and business survey.
Base: Tooting = 512/150, Ball Hill = 489/78, London Road = 405/87.

An open question in the street-user and business surveys asked for suggestions as to how the street might be improved. In both cases, around 15% of respondents suggested that efforts should be made to keep the streets cleaner and litter-free. In Tooting, however, there was a stark contrast between the perceptions of businesses and street users, with only 8% of the former group suggesting this type of improvement, compared with 30% of the latter.

Strong concerns over the negative effects of road traffic

While most respondents were concerned about the physical state of their mixed-use streets, and the poor levels of public amenity, the most significant problem that street-users and residents identified with their local high street was the volume of road traffic (Figure 5.7). Here, across the three roads, between 70% and 90% of respondents considered this to be a major or minor problem.

Figure 5.7: Proportion of street users and businesses identifying traffic-related issues as a major or minor problem

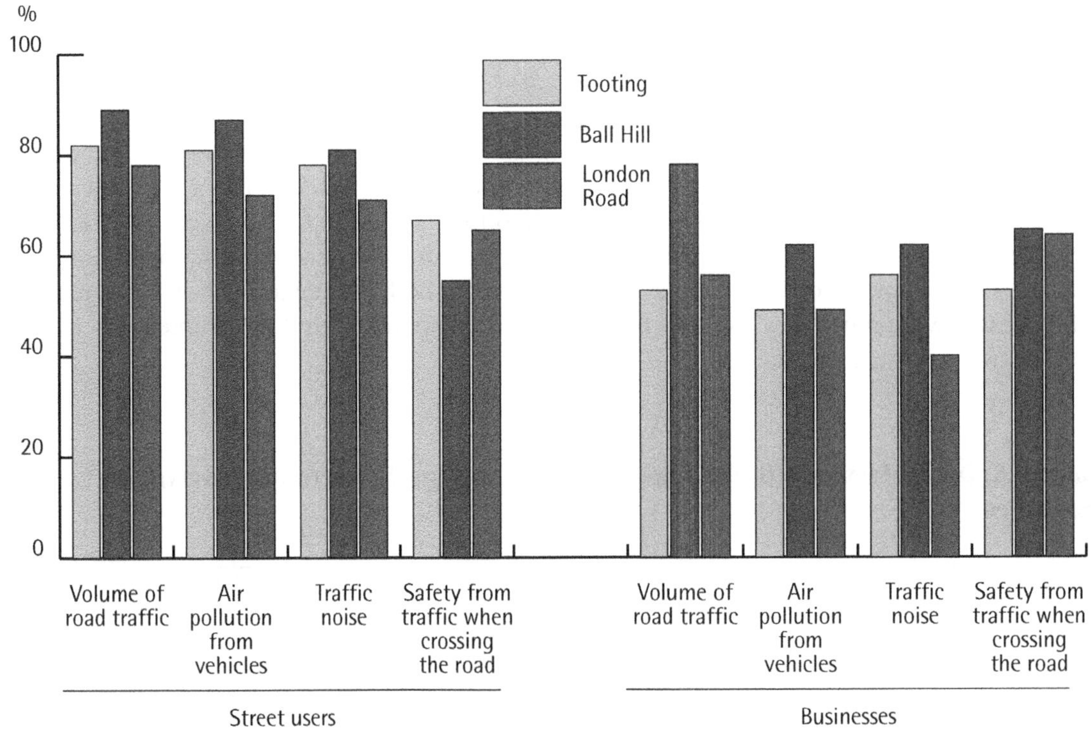

Source: street-user survey and business surveys.
Base: Tooting = 512/150, Ball Hill = 489/78, London Road = 405/87.

Air pollution and traffic noise were also recognised as a significant problem, but respondents were less likely to consider them a 'major' problem. Interestingly, businesses were generally less likely to feel that traffic issues were a problem, except in relation to traffic volumes through Ball Hill.

The problems of traffic congestion and poor air quality in Ball Hill provided the initial points of concern for proposing action among professionals in Ball Hill. The council was concerned about the level of pollution and traffic delays through the area, and had substantial funding to improve the speed and reliability of bus services and to take on radical ideas to improve traffic congestion and pollution levels.

Findings from the community street audits

The community street audits concentrated on the visual appearance of the streets, and the ease of moving around the area on foot.

Poor general appearance

The community street audits reported low overall levels of satisfaction with the appearance of the three streets. Focus group respondents in Tooting also bemoaned the unattractiveness of their area, stating they would like to 'give it a good clean'.

Visual observations found that all the case study sites suffered from poorly coordinated and obtrusive shop fronts and fascias. These detracted, in some cases, from the regularity and relative attractiveness of the building elevation above.

Left: Tooting: uncoordinated fascias detract from appearance of street

Right: Ball Hill: commercial frontage dominates street scene

One common concern was over the presence of buildings in a poor state of repair. This included buildings with a poor level of maintenance, establishments with boarded up windows and premises with graffiti and fly posters on their walls – all contributing to a general impression of neglect. This not only reduced the attractiveness of the area, but could also give the impression of a place that would be unsafe to visit at night.

London Road: an untidy wall with graffiti

Another common theme was dissatisfaction with the amount of greenery in the areas. Tooting had previously planted trees, which had died as a result of traffic pollution, while London Road has some poorly maintained planters outside the chemist. It was felt by participants in the street audit that both these areas would benefit from the introduction of more vegetation and soft landscaping. Flowers and planters outside shops could improve the visual appearance of the frontages.

Participants from the Ball Hill and London Road street audits were both concerned about the pavements, which were described as broken and in disrepair.

Pavement in disrepair

Tree root pulling up paving in London Road

Issues were also raised about the lack of consistency in the layout and design of paving in Tooting and London Road, with London Road described as having a 'patchwork quilt of materials'. This problem is exacerbated in the Tooting area, where two separate organisations have the remit for maintaining adjoining areas (see Chapter 6).

London Road's pavement – a patchwork of materials

Too much street furniture

Participants from the community street audits felt that there was often too much street furniture on the footway, and that items such as railings, phone boxes and bus stops were poorly placed in the middle of the pavement, causing obstructions and congestion on the already narrow footways.

Railings almost a metre from the kerb

Phonebox narrows the pavement

Figure 5.8 demonstrates how much of the footway around the Broadway junction in Tooting is dominated by street furniture. The green pixels – which show where there is one piece of street furniture per 2m² – reflect the extent of guardrail hemming in the pavement. There are also yellow and red pixels – which show where there are two or three items per 2m² – concentrated on the narrowest points of the pavement, particularly on Upper Tooting Road. The pedestrian refuges in the roads are particularly dense with street furniture. They are already quite narrow, and the use of guardrails creates a very confined space, especially with the inclusion of additional posts with a variety of functions.

Figure 5.8: Street furniture density around Tooting Broadway junction

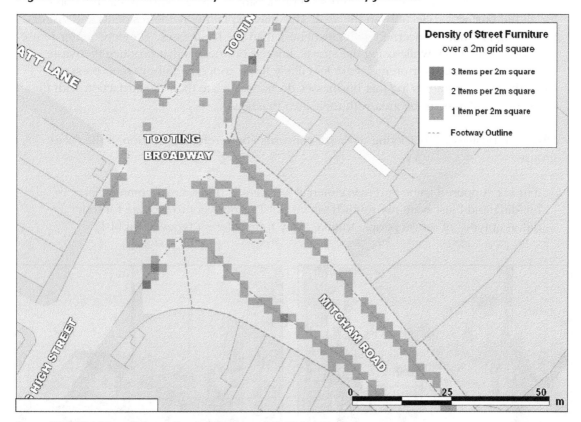

Source: TfL AIMS database. Ordnance Survey. © Crown copyright. All rights reserved.

As well as finding the streets overcrowded with signage and other clutter, the street audits recorded that much of the furniture was 'shabby', uncoordinated and poorly maintained. Certain items of street furniture, such as pedestrian guardrails around pelican crossings, tend to get damaged or wear out more frequently than others. Such items can be difficult to repair, as they require one lane of the road to be cordoned off. For these reasons, it was suggested that councils should be more selective in their choice of street furniture.

Concerns about litter and lack of street cleanliness

The community street audits highlighted specific concerns about cleanliness. In Ball Hill, the lack of litter bins along the length of the street was raised as a problem. Those that did exist were criticised for allowing refuse to blow out when full because they had no lids.

On London Road, despite the proliferation of takeaway restaurants, criticism of a lack of cleanliness was levelled only at the new student residence, with students suspected of discarding takeaway wrappings on the pavements around the area. There had been a problem with litter along the length of the road from all of the takeaway establishments, but this has since been remedied with the introduction of a street cleaner to the area. There is now only a problem on match days at the local football ground, when the use of local takeaway restaurants soars.

Tooting suffers particularly from the problem of refuse bags from commercial businesses being left out on the pavement waiting for collection. In addition to adversely affecting the image of the street, they narrow the pavement and cause an obstruction.

This problem of refuse sacks being left on the street is more of an issue in Tooting than in the other areas for two reasons. First, there are no back entrances to many of the premises

77

in Tooting where bags can be left, and second, no single waste company has the contract for all the business collections in the area. This may explain why the residents and visitors to Tooting are more concerned with cleanliness than the businesses. They encounter refuse bags on a daily basis while using the streets, but the businesses that produce the waste and leave it outside their premises are less likely to be concerned about their presence. Nevertheless, it is interesting that businesses do not associate their dissatisfaction with the levels of cleanliness in the area with their own practices.

However, businesses in Tooting did raise concerns about refuse collection in the focus groups:

'I'm not supposed to be an Environmental Act person. I just run a commercial building and I just want my rubbish taken. But I've now got to arrange for four different types of refuse people to take away four different types of rubbish!'

Bin bags being left out on the footway are a constant problem in Tooting

Use of forecourts

The shops in Tooting and Ball Hill display an array of goods and signs on the forecourts outside their premises. There are varying opinions about this practice, with some street audit participants believing the stalls add colour and character, with others feeling they make the area look untidy.

One problem with shop-front displays is that they narrow the footway, causing obstructions and congestion. Participants of the Ball Hill community street audit were particularly concerned about how this affected the safe passage of older and disabled people. This is considered further in Chapter 6.

In the Tooting focus groups, participants felt that there had been an increase in the number of people trading on the pavement in recent years. Nobody seemed to be strongly against this practice, and some people felt that it added to the atmosphere of the street. One businesses owner commented:

'I think it looks nice. It's going like the Southall feel and the appeal. Their pavements are not big by any margin, but they have stalls and tables that go out. All the noises, the smells and the colour, when you walk down it, it's a nice shopping feel. I think it's a big attraction.'

Shop-front displays narrow the pavement   Stalls add interest and vibrancy

Community visions and aspirations

In two of the case study areas (Coventry and Tooting), in conjunction with this project the local authorities held a stakeholder design workshop concerning the future of the local high street. The workshop in Tooting reinforced and elaborated the perceptions of businesses and residents discussed earlier in this chapter and highlighted the potential for making improvements to the public realm.

Proposals that were considered and developed included improvements to the streetscape around the Broadway junction, using contemporary ideas such as removing the guardrails and redundant street furniture, and developing a more convivial public space on the wide footway in front of Primark, for example, by including an historic memorial. The concept of relocating the bus turnaround in Mitcham Road and introducing a Sunday market was also mooted. The town centre manager has expressed enthusiasm for subsequently taking these ideas forward.

Tooting Urban Design Workshop

The Coventry workshop was initiated as a result of conflict between the council and local businesses, as is described in Chapter 6 (pages 103-104).

Summary

This chapter has focused on mixed-use streets as places; it was not possible to interview the drivers and passengers who use the streets as links. Customers interviewed on the street generally liked their local mixed-use street; it provided local identity and they were very satisfied with the range and quality of local shops/businesses, and the friendliness of the local staff. The smallest centre, Ball Hill, had the highest approval ratings – as it did among businesses.

However, in other respects, the streets were seen as being much less attractive. They generally had the air of being neglected, due to the presence of litter and graffiti and the poor state of repair of some buildings. People were also concerned about the lack of provision of basic public amenities. In particular, our surveys found that a lack of public toilets was a key area of dissatisfaction, as was a lack of public seating.

The high volumes of road traffic arising from the link function of mixed-use streets, and the consequential air pollution from vehicles and traffic noise, are perceived to be serious problems among street users in all three areas, detracting considerably from the experience of visiting the local high street.

In the three community street audits, high levels of dissatisfaction were recorded with the appearance of the streets, the state of the buildings, the design and condition of the pavements, the extent of street clutter and the limited provision of greenery. Streets can often be cluttered with poorly placed, badly maintained street furniture. This creates obstacles and contributes to congestion on the footway.

In common with concerns expressed by local residents and businesses, the auditors identified litter and street cleanliness as problems. Tooting has a particular problem with refuse sacks being left on the footway at all times of the day, because of the large number of private waste contractors operating in the area.

Many of the forecourts in Tooting and Ball Hill are used by businesses to display their goods. Street users expressed varying opinions about the presence of these stalls. While they add welcome colour and a sense of vitality, a key concern is that in certain places they narrow the footway and can cause an obstruction. Such problems are further addressed in Chapter 6.

The Urban Design Workshop demonstrated the willingness of local stakeholders to develop visions and set out their aspirations for the area, as a basis for exploring innovative solutions to these problems.

6

Issues confronting mixed-use streets

The previous chapters have demonstrated the richness, density and diversity of activities to be found on mixed-use streets, all taking place in a relatively confined space. Inevitably, this results in varying degrees of pressure, tension and conflict, both in terms of competition among street users for space or capacity and the compatibility of different types of street activities.

This chapter explores some of these tensions and conflicts, from the perspectives of different street users. It examines the overall demand for link and place space, the conflicting pressures on footway use and the conflicts between the space required for street furniture and pedestrian activity. Attention then turns to the carriageway, looking at conflicting pressures on the use of the kerbside, and the restrictions on through vehicle movement caused by illegal parking and buses setting down/picking up at bus stops.

The chapter then considers issues of safety and security on mixed-use streets, by investigating patterns of traffic accidents, and the incidence of street crime. Finally, it looks at the overall management of the street, and the involvement of street users in their planning, design and operation.

Pressures for link and place space

An indication of the balance of pressure to accommodate link and place activities on mixed-use streets can be gauged from the relative volumes of motor vehicles and pedestrians. Table 6.1 shows pedestrian numbers as a percentage of the total numbers of vehicles and pedestrians, on a weekday between 08.00 and 19.00, in the three case study areas.

Here we can observe large daytime differences between the three case study sites. On London Road, only 20% of all the movements along the street are on foot, in an area that is characterised more by night-time activity. This rises to 40% on Walsgrave Road in Ball Hill, which is predominantly a daytime centre, and to an average of 55% in Tooting on the two main streets, where there is a higher pedestrian than vehicle flow. The highest figures in Tooting are for Upper Tooting Road on a Saturday, when pedestrians make up 61% of the total movement.

Table 6.1: Pedestrian flow as a percentage of vehicle and pedestrian flow

	%
Ball Hill	40
London Road	20
Tooting	55

Source: CCTV analysis.

Hence, the relative volumes of pedestrian and vehicle movements, and the nature and degree of conflict between link and place uses, vary considerably from one mixed-use street and one time period to another.

Conflicting footway pressures

Mixed-use streets often suffer from pedestrian congestion, particularly where the footway is narrow, or there is intrusive street furniture. This issue was explored both in the street-user and business surveys, and via an analysis of CCTV data.

Perceptions of footway congestion

The street user and business surveys asked respondents if they felt there were any problems in moving along the pavement;[7] the results are shown in Figure 6.1. In Tooting and Ball Hill, over 50% of street users considered this to be a problem, but only 25% in London Road. This echoes the findings of the street audits, since in London Road no pinch points were observed, and the volumes of pedestrian movement were lowest.

In all the three areas, businesses seemed to be much less aware of the problems people experience in moving along the footway. In each case, levels of concern among businesses are approximately half those expressed by street users.

Figure 6.1: Contrasting street-user and business views about difficulties in moving along the pavement

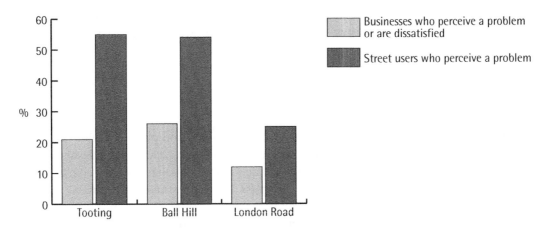

Legend:
- Businesses who perceive a problem or are dissatisfied
- Street users who perceive a problem

Source: street-user and business surveys.
Base: Tooting = 512/150; Ball Hill = 489/78; London Road = 405/87.

Pinch points on the footway

The community street audit identified a number of pinch points in the Tooting Broadway area, as shown in Figure 6.2, mainly caused by poorly placed or unnecessary street furniture. This has the effect of funnelling pedestrian movement into narrow gaps and in some instances channelling it along routes that are not the most direct and are often undesirable.

---

[7] Tooting businesses were asked how satisfied they were with 'ease of movement along the pavement'. In Ball Hill and London Road, the percentages equate to the percentages of businesses that perceived a problem (minor and major) with 'ease of moving along the pavement'.

Figure 6.2: Pinch points in the Tooting Broadway area

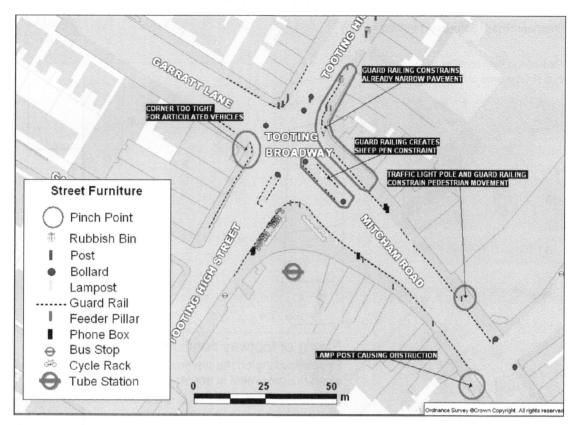

Source: TfL AIMS database, plus local surveys.

One of the most restrictive features that hems in pedestrians and limits their freedom of movement is the extensive use of guardrails. Mitcham Road is an extreme case, as illustrated above, where 88% of the footway within 100 metres of the Broadway junction has guardrails installed.

Where pedestrian flows are high, and the footway has been narrowed by street furniture and other obstructions, pedestrian congestion can result. The Danish public space architect, Jan Gehl, has identified a maximum pedestrian flow of 13 persons per metre per minute (p/m/min) above which serious pedestrian congestion can arise.

In Tooting, this value is regularly exceeded at some locations. One example was observed from the CCTV analysis on Mitcham Road adjacent to a bus stop and shelter, where a congested pinch point results in pedestrians regularly walking in the road to bypass the bottleneck, as shown in Figure 6.3.

On average, 29 people per minute walk along the 3.8 metres wide pavement at the peak flow between 13.00 and 14.00 on a Saturday. The bus shelter, including people standing waiting, can reduce this width to 2.1 metres, or less. This results in a density of movement of around 14-15 p/m/min, and the consequences are shown in the video footage.

A similar problem was observed in Ball Hill, on a busy and relatively narrow section of public footway, where there was a telephone box close to the carriageway and shop displays on the adjacent private forecourt. Here, on a Saturday, pedestrian flows frequently exceeded this critical value.

Figure 6.3: Consequences of inadequate footway capacity in Tooting

Mitcham Road, Saturday 18/06/05

Pedestrian flow conflicts in the
bus shelter area outside KFC

11:00   Photo of Plan1.

13:28   Photo of Plan2.

15:06   Photo of Plan2.

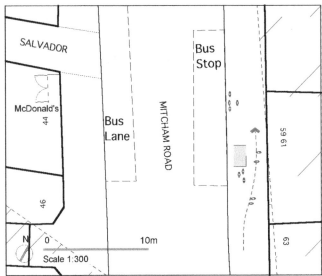

Plan 1 of footway conflicts
People walking on the pavement
when the pavement is not crowded.

CCTV

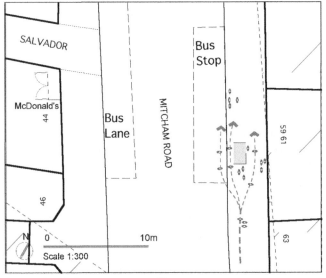

Plan 2 of footway conflicts
People walking in the narrow space
between the bus shelters and road,
and along the road when the pavement
is crowded.

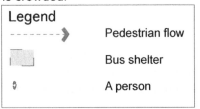
CCTV

Number of pedestrians on Mitcham Road on a Saturday on
both directions (KFC side of road)

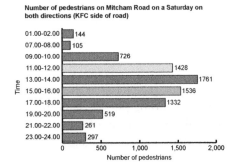

Time	Number of pedestrians
01.00-02.00	144
07.00-08.00	105
09.00-10.00	726
11.00-12.00	1428
13.00-14.00	1761
15.00-16.00	1536
17.00-18.00	1332
19.00-20.00	519
21.00-22.00	261
23.00-24.00	297

Number of pedestrians

Legend

- - - → Pedestrian flow

Bus shelter

A person

Source: CCTV footage; Ordnance Survey, © Crown copyright, all rights reserved.

Pressures on kerbside use

Requirements for loading

A high proportion of businesses rely on kerbside loading, and most report problems with loading/unloading and access by service vehicles.

Figure 6.4 shows the extent to which businesses report using different locations for their loading/unloading activities; responses at each site total more than 100%, as they may rely on more than one type of location.

The most commonly mentioned location is the mixed-use street itself, referred to by over 70% of businesses in Ball Hill and around 60% in Tooting and London Road. Businesses in the latter two case studies report making relatively more use of side roads; off-street provision is mentioned by fewer than 20% of respondents in any of the areas.

Figure 6.4: Places where loading is carried out by businesses

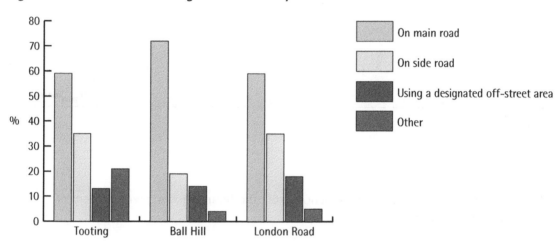

Source: business surveys.
Base: Tooting = 150, Ball Hill = 78, London Road = 87.

To what extent does loading cause problems for businesses? Around 60% of the businesses interviewed reported problems with loading and service access in Ball Hill and Tooting, with only 45% doing so in London Road – probably because of the different mix of businesses on that street. This arises from the limited kerb space on mixed-use streets, and competing demands from other kerbside uses.

Competing kerbside uses

There are many demands placed on the limited kerb space available on mixed-use streets. Figure 6.5 illustrates the different ways in which the kerb space is allocated within 200 metres of the Tooting Broadway junction on the two case study streets. Some of these differences on the two roads are due to the different sets of regulations that apply in the Tooting area. Tooting High Street is on the Transport for London Road Network and is a 'red route', while the other roads are under borough control where standard national yellow line regulations apply.

Figure 6.5: Use of kerb space in the vicinity of Tooting Broadway

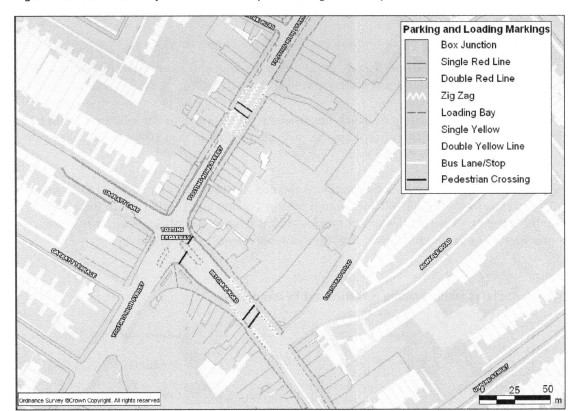

Source: TfL AIMS database.

Apart from the space taken by the junction itself, the figure shows a wide variety of regulated uses, including:

- double red lines (indicating no stopping at any time);
- single red lines (no stopping during the working day);
- space for pedestrian crossings;
- white zigzag lines (no stopping on the approaches to pedestrian crossings);
- off-peak loading bays;
- bus stop areas;
- single yellow lines (no parking during the day, loading only);
- yellow box junctions;
- side-road entrances.

The balance of allocation of kerb space can vary quite significantly from one street to another, due to differences in width, the number of bus routes, types of frontage and so on. It can also be quite different on opposite sides of the same section of street, and can differ between peak and off-peak periods.

Figure 6.6 illustrates each of these points, by comparing kerbside use on Mitcham Road and Upper Tooting Road, by time of day, and on each side of the street in the central section of Ball Hill.

Figure 6.6: Differences in allocation of kerb space, by area, time of day and side of the street in Ball Hill and Tooting

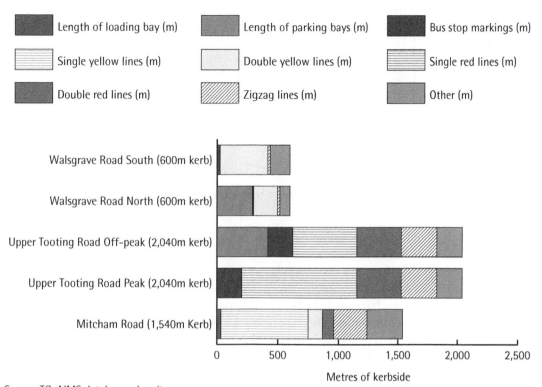

Source: TfL AIMS database, plus site surveys.

More specifically, we can observe that:

- On Walsgrave Road, Ball Hill, around 40% of the north kerbside is allocated to parking, but there is none on the south side.
- On Upper Tooting Road, around 20% of the kerb space is provided for off-peak parking, but none is provided at peak times. Outside red route hours (7am to 7pm) about half the street is available for parking.
- Mitcham Road is not a red route, and has a very different allocation of kerb space within the same district centre. Here there is no provision for on-street parking – although, again, around half the street is available for parking outside the working day.

Conflicts with through traffic

Illegal parking and loading

Illegal parking and loading can block a traffic lane and considerably reduce traffic capacity. On busy main roads, space is usually provided on the carriageway for vehicles to bypass to the left of a right-turning traffic queue, by preventing kerbside parking and loading in the vicinity. When vehicles do park illegally in such locations (shown in the photograph on the next page), traffic can back up on the main road and a queue develops quite quickly. This can take a considerable time to clear even after the offending vehicle has moved on.

Vehicles delayed by right-turning traffic due to illegal parking

However, illegal parking does not always delay moving traffic. On the south side of Walsgrave Road in Ball Hill, for example, there is no provision for kerbside parking and loading, and cars and vans frequently park illegally, partly on the footway, for periods ranging from a few minutes to more than an hour. An example, from around midday on a Saturday, is shown in the photograph below. There was no evidence from the CCTV analysis that this caused problems for the relatively small number of pedestrians on the wide footway, nor for moving traffic. The local traders have asked that some legal parking be provided along this section of street.

Example of an illegally parked vehicle in Ball Hill

Traffic delays caused by buses

While buses play a significant role in providing a sustainable and socially inclusive method of travel to mixed-use streets from further afield, in some situations buses were observed to significantly delay link traffic flows.

Ball Hill

Traders in Ball Hill reported that traffic delays were caused by buses waiting at certain bus stops for passengers to board and alight; this affected not only general traffic movement, but also other buses.

Video analysis showed that westbound buses sometimes delay traffic when picking up/ setting down passengers at the stop to the west of the pelican crossing in the central section of the high street, as shown in the photograph below. On average, there are 22 buses per hour in this direction.

Traffic delays caused by buses at a stop in Ball Hill

When there is no traffic coming in the opposite direction, vehicles use the other side of the road to overtake the standing bus. However, if there is oncoming traffic, they usually wait. In these circumstances, the average delay for each waiting vehicle was observed to be 18 seconds.

Occasionally, while one bus is using the westbound stop, a queue of more buses develops behind. This clogs up the road and causes further delay for all vehicles. During the period of observation, there were three occasions with multiple buses at the stop. When this occurs, the delay for other motor vehicles is much greater, of the order of one to two minutes.

Tooting

Problems resulting from multiple buses stopping at the same time were more frequently observed in the CCTV analysis of Mitcham Road, Tooting, which has 10 high frequency bus routes and around 160 buses per hour, in the two directions. High volumes of bus passengers boarding and alighting can result in buses spending several minutes at these stops in peak times. Examples of the resulting traffic delays caused by buses spending extended periods at stops are shown in Figure 6.7.

Figure 6.7: Delays caused by multiple buses attempting to pick up passengers at the same time, in Mitcham Road, Tooting

Conflicts around bus stops, Saturday 18/06/05

13:56:41 Six buses causing traffic delays.

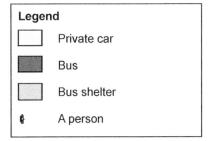

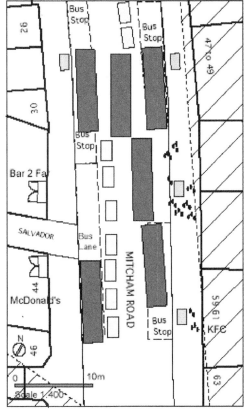

Plan view of traffic conflicts.

CCTV

Sequence of events blocking traffic movement

13:53:59
Second bus squeezes in between first and third buses.

13:54:44
First bus departs, but the second still protrudes and blocks other vehicles.

In the top photograph and diagram, three buses are picking up passengers southbound, with a fourth bus trying to overtake them, while two buses pick up passengers on the opposite side of the road. Due to the flow of general traffic northbound, this prevents all traffic movement southbound.

The second sequence of pictures shows the second bus back trying to squeeze into the kerbside between a double and single decker bus to pick up passengers. As a consequence, its rear is protruding into the carriageway. When the first bus moves off, the second bus is still stationary and picking up passengers, so remains protruding into the carriageway, thereby preventing other buses and general road traffic from passing the stop.

Safety and security

Traffic accidents

Traffic accidents can represent a significant problem on mixed-use streets, due to the high concentrations of vehicles and pedestrians carrying out a broad range of manoeuvres and activities in close proximity. Analysis in all three case studies found concentrations of accidents at major road junctions, with secondary peaks in some cases close to bus stops – where people attempt to cross the street informally, to access or alight from a bus. There was also some evidence of small clusters of accidents around night-time activities.

The Tooting case study presents the most complex street environment, and is examined in more detail here. Figure 6.8 shows the distribution of accidents on Mitcham and Upper Tooting Road, on the approaches to Tooting Broadway junction, over a three-year period.

Figure 6.8: Traffic accidents in Tooting

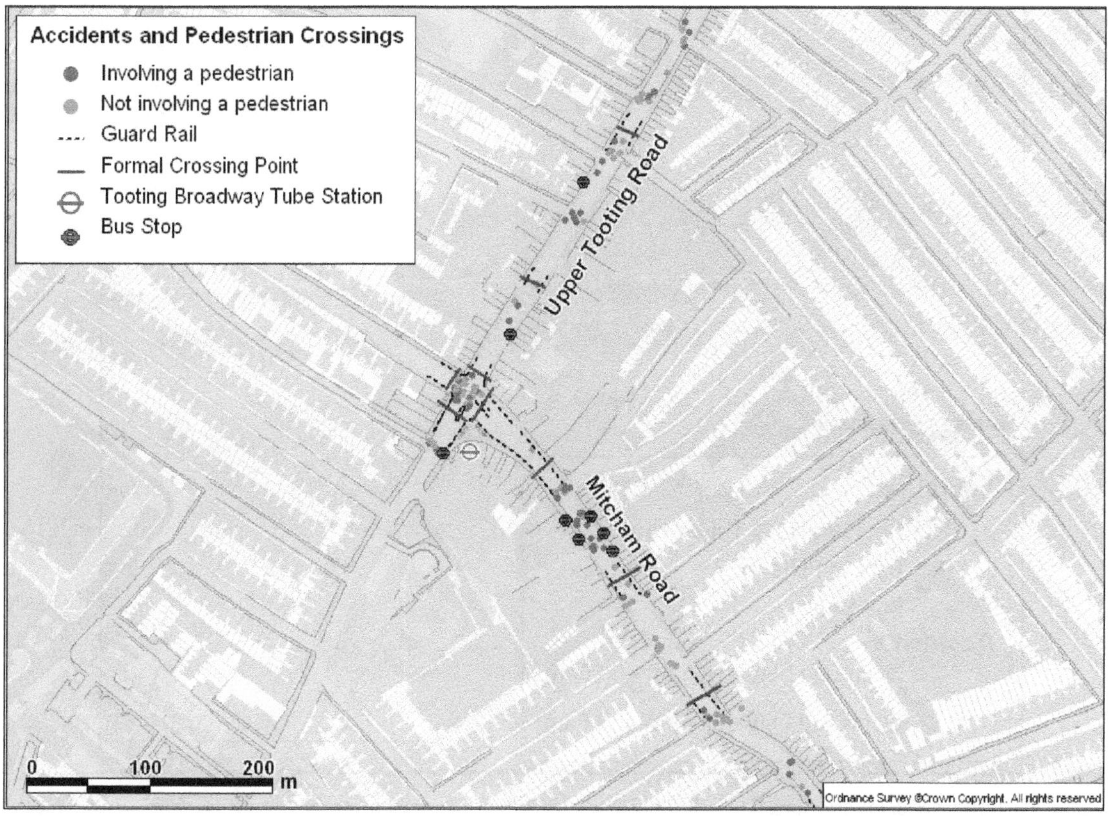

Source: TfL traffic accidents statistics.

There is a major cluster of vehicle–vehicle and vehicle–pedestrian accidents around the Broadway, and smaller clusters at several of the other road junctions. In addition, on Mitcham Road, there is large a cluster of vehicle–pedestrian accidents that occur away from the formal crossing points, in the vicinity of the bus stops. Pedestrians crossing at these points away from the formal crossings seem to be at more risk of an accident. Particularly in Tooting, not only was there a large accident cluster around the bus stops on Mitcham

Road, but the video survey also showed many near misses, as people either rushed across the road to board a bus, or stepped out into the carriageway from behind a bus, while being largely obscured from the view of vehicle drivers by other buses.

A possible association with the location of night-time activities in Tooting can be seen in Figure 6.9.

Figure 6.9: Accidents involving pedestrians by time of day, in relation to the location of night-time land-use activity

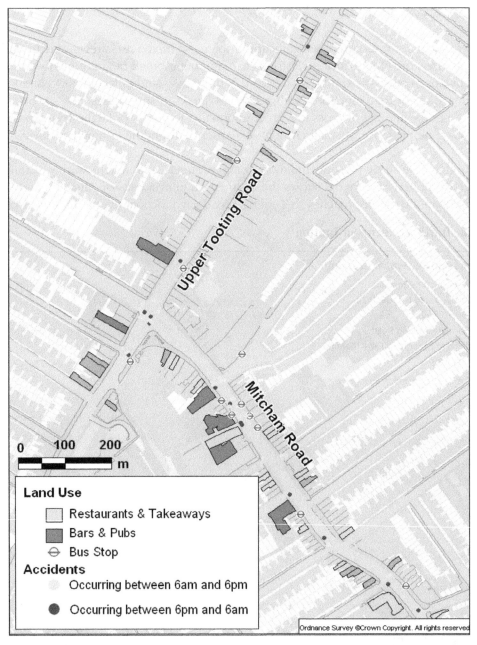

Source: TfL traffic accidents statistics.

This highlights the location of restaurants, takeaway shops, bars and public houses. Here the accidents shown are only those involving pedestrians. While the majority of pedestrian accidents occur during the day (6am to 6pm), there is a small cluster of night-time accidents on Mitcham Road outside two public houses, and again in the vicinity of the bus stops.

This analysis suggests a possible relationship between bus stop location and pedestrian accidents at busy transport interchange points that has not previously been highlighted in the literature. This probably results from a combination of people rushing between transport modes, and the obscuring of traffic and pedestrians by the buses themselves.

In Ball Hill, accident levels were low compared with Tooting. The focal point of the Ball Hill shopping area, Clay Lane junction, is where the vast majority of accidents occur. Most are during daylight conditions, with more on the western edge of the junction; one of the accidents occurred during rain. Note that only one recorded accident involved a pedestrian away from the Clay Lane junction – and this was in the vicinity of a westbound bus stop.

In the case of London Road, there are clusters of vehicle-only accidents at the junction of London Road and the inner ring road, and at the other major traffic intersections, but – compared with the other two streets – pedestrian casualties are relatively light. Two of the six occur in the vicinity of bus stops, but the numbers involved are too small to have any confidence in any association on this street between pedestrian accidents and bus stop locations.

Street intimidation and street crime

Problems on the street

The street-user surveys asked respondents whether they thought that 'personal safety on foot at night' was a major problem on their mixed-use street and surrounding area. Businesses were asked a similar question, as to whether they thought that this had an effect on reducing the attractiveness of the street to their customers. The responses for those who indicated 'a major problem' and 'a strong effect', respectively, are shown in Figure 6.10, for each of the case study areas.

The levels of street-user and business concern were generally low (at between 20% and 25%), broadly similar, and varied little across the three areas. The closest agreement between the two groups was in Tooting, while in Ball Hill (where there is little evening business activity), street users were more likely to be concerned than businesses and in London Road (where there is a strong evening and night-time provision), businesses were relatively more concerned than the street users interviewed.

Figure 6.10: Street–user and business concerns about personal safety on foot at night (percentage identifying major problem/major effect on businesses)

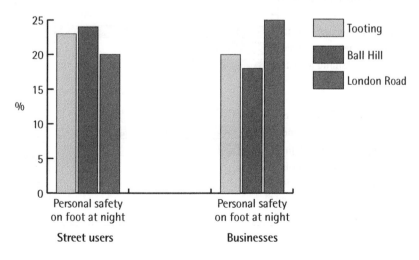

Source: street-user and business surveys.
Base: Tooting = 512/150; Ball Hill = 489/78; London Road = 405/87

Respondents to the on-street survey were then asked more specifically about whether they personally felt pressured or threatened by other people on the street, either at night or during the day. Overall, 23% of street users in Tooting and Ball Hill reported feeling some sort of threat/pressure, while in London Road this figure rose to 34%. Here there were particularly strong differences between men (at 26%) and women (48%).

One possible explanation for the higher incidence of concern on London Road may be the high proportion of street users who were interviewed at night. However, closer examination of the data shows that, with the exception of people aged over 60 years, the proportion expressing concern was found to be *lower* in the evening sample than in the daytime sample. This suggests that the source of many people's concern may have been associated with a group of alcoholics and drug users who regularly congregated on one section of London Road during the day.

Those respondents who reported feeling threatened or pressured were then asked what was the cause of their concern. Figure 6.11 shows the responses from all three areas' on-street sample.

While the comments are specific to the individual areas, common concerns were observed. In Tooting and Ball Hill, the main way these threats/pressures were expressed was as 'youth on the streets hanging around'. However, in London Road, the main threat/pressure was 'drunks/drug addicts', as previously noted.

The second most stated threats were more generic, for example, 'general feeling of unease at night' and 'street crime/fear of crime'. Interestingly, there were no significant differences between genders concerning the nature of the threats on the street in Tooting. Residents had a more negative outlook in Ball Hill and London Road, where they were more likely to feel threatened than visitors.

Figure 6.11: Most commonly mentioned causes of being threatened/pressured

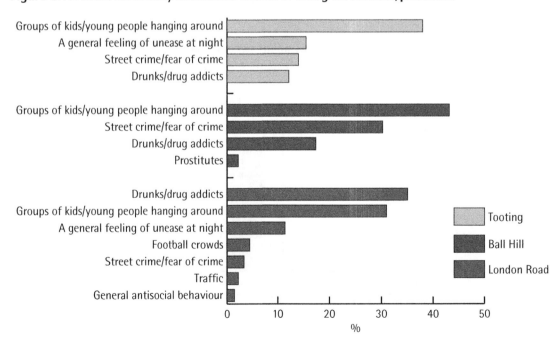

Source: street-user survey.
Base: Tooting =120, Ball Hill = 110, London Road = 138.

Similar concerns were expressed by Tooting residents in the focus groups:

'It's intimidating sometimes to see a lot of people and you're just one person and you're just trying to get through them, but they can be quite intimidating.' (Younger resident, female)

'It's getting better, but there's the culture of walking gangs. You pass them, and it's not that you're frightened of them, but you have to be aware, no matter what. You could be minding your own business, but you still have to be aware of them, at all times.' (Older resident, male)

Problems affecting businesses

Business respondents were asked a series of questions about the types of crime and antisocial behaviour that might affect them and their staff. Responses are shown in Figure 6.12. Up to a quarter of businesses reported some sort of problem in Tooting and Ball Hill, but only up to 15% in London Road. The nature of the problems experienced seems to vary from one area to another. In Tooting, the problems affecting most businesses were shoplifting and verbal assaults towards staff; in Ball Hill they were robberies/break-ins and shoplifting, and on London Road robberies/break-ins and graffiti/vandalism.

Figure 6.12: Percentage of businesses indicating that certain types of crime and antisocial behaviour were a major problem for them

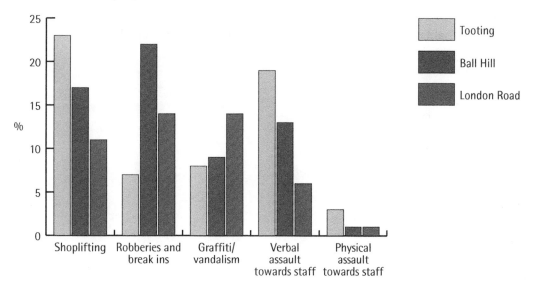

Source: business surveys.
Base: Tooting = 150, Ball Hill = 78, London Road = 87.

General crime-related problems in the area

In Tooting and London Road, the police were able to provide a general overview of crime and antisocial behaviour in different parts of the study areas. These schematic diagrams are shown in Figures 6.13 and 6.14.

Figure 6.13: Hot spots of street crime and antisocial behaviour in Tooting

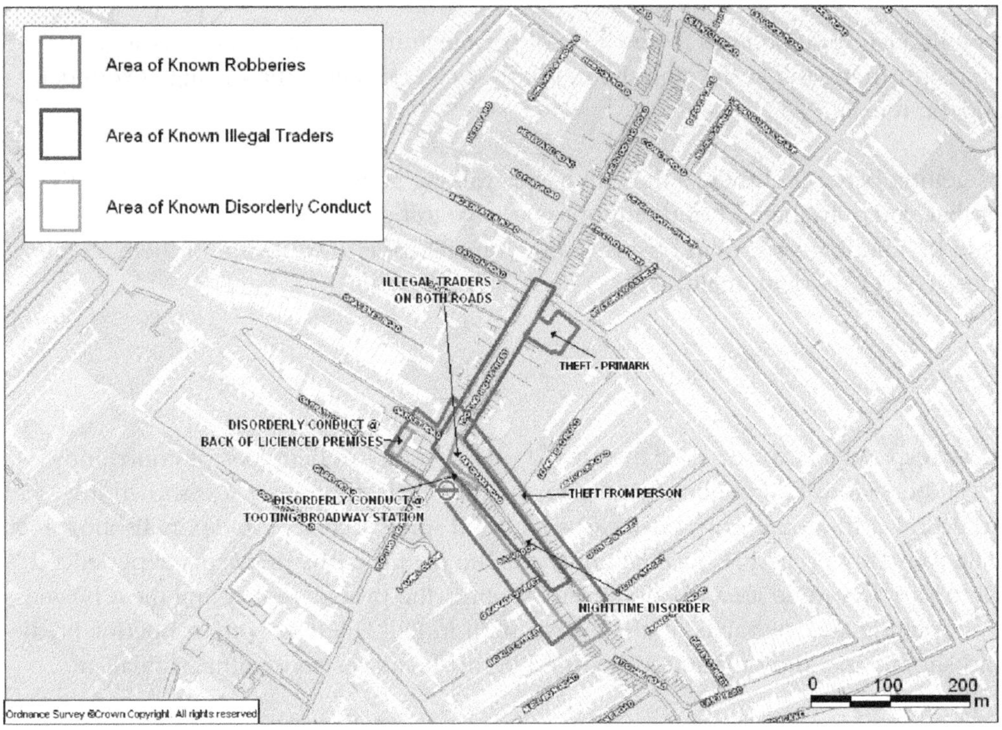

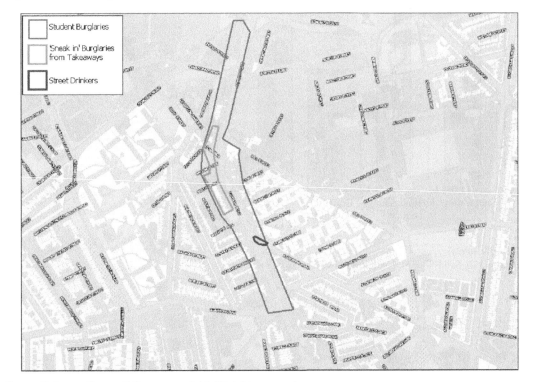

Area of Known Robberies
Area of Known Illegal Traders
Area of Known Disorderly Conduct
ILLEGAL TRADERS ON BOTH ROADS
THEFT - PRIMARK
DISORDERLY CONDUCT @ BACK OF LICIENCED PREMISES
DISORDERLY CONDUCT @ TOOTING BROADWAY STATION
THEFT FROM PERSON
NIGHTTIME DISORDER
0
100
200
m
Ordnance Survey ©Crown Copyright All rights reserved

Source: Ordnance Survey. © Crown copyright. All rights reserved.

In the case of Tooting, this highlights several types of street-related crime at, and on the approaches to, Tooting Broadway junction, which is a focus of pedestrian activity.

Figure 6.14: Hot spots of street crime and antisocial behaviour in London Road

Student Burglaries
'Sneak in' Burglaries from Takeaways
Street Drinkers

Source: Ordnance Survey. © Crown copyright. All rights reserved.

In the London Road area, there is a hot spot associated with street drinking, and problems associated with theft from takeaway restaurants. The high student residential population is also vulnerable to theft.

Managing streets: overlapping responsibilities and uncertainties

Responsibilities for street planning, design, management and operation

Many agencies are involved in some aspect of the non-commercial operation of the street, ranging from local authority traffic engineers and planners, environmental services and building control, to the police and private crime prevention agencies, as well as those responsible for providing and maintaining street furniture and street utilities. Together these influence the planning, design, management and operation of mixed-use streets.

Some agencies operate locally (for example, local government authorities); others operate regionally (for example, health authorities), nationally or internationally (for example, the Royal Mail, and most telecommunications companies). Several organisations are in the public sector, but increasing numbers of private sector providers are becoming involved, due to both the outsourcing and privatisation of public services, and to the growing number and range of commercial services on offer in mixed-use streets.

Using the classification of the components of the street set out in Figure 1.1, Tables 6.2 and 6.3 list some of the features to be found on mixed-use streets and the associated functions that support these streets, and show which agencies are responsible for each one, for the contrasting cases of Tooting and London Road.

As a comparison of these tables shows, the basic organisational structures are different in the two areas, particularly among the public sector agencies, and there are also differences in terms of which agency has responsibility for a particular feature or function.

For example, in Tooting, most of the highway management services on borough roads are the responsibility of Wandsworth Borough Council's Department of Technical Services, while on Transport for London's (TfL) roads, responsibility lies with TfL's Street Management Services divisions. In London Road, the work is split between Transport and Highway Services, and the Street Force team, which deals with a broad range of street furniture and highway maintenance issues. In the case of street crime, the existence of an underground station at Tooting Broadway brings in the interests of the British Transport Police, alongside the Metropolitan Police Authority, and the local community safety partnership.

This complexity of the administrative and organisational structures involved in the myriad aspects of the functioning of mixed-use streets is very confusing for street-user groups, and in some situations makes it very difficult to coordinate activities and facilitate significant improvements to the street environment.

Planning, legislation and design issues

Discussions with businesses, local residents and street agencies revealed a number of concerns and confusions about how streets are planned, managed and operated. Some of the key points raised are summarised below.

Uncertainties about ownership

Mixed-use streets contain buildings and many other structures (some built decades or centuries ago) that are owned by a very wide range of agencies and individuals, and it can often be difficult to track down who has ownership and responsibility for them. In the case of buildings, in particular, there may be an occupier, tenant, landlord and the ultimate

97

Table 6.2: Agency responsibilities for aspects of streets in Tooting

Bold = Interview undertaken with member(s) of department

Aspect		Town centre Manager/ Economic Development Unit	Dept of Technical Services	Dept of Leisure and Amenities Services	Environmental Services	Planning Service	Housing Department	Community Safety Division	Metropolitan Police	British Transport Police	Business/ home owner	Tenant/ landlord/ freeholder	Housing Management Agent (Co-op/RMO)	London Fire and Emergency Planning Authority	Association of London Government	Royal Mail	External contractors	Utility companies	Street Management Services	London Buses	London Underground
Street																					
Economic development of town centre	Red route	✓																			
	Non–red route																				
Underground station	Red route																				
	Non–red route																				✓
Environmental issues	Red route			✓																	
	Non–red route																				
Planning	Red route					✓															
	Non–red route																				
Crime	Red route																				
	Non–red route							✓	✓	✓									✓	✓	
Advertising	Red route					✓															
	Non–red route																		✓		
Graffiti removal	Red route						✓												✓		
	Non–red route																				
Issuing and enforcing trading	Red route																				
	Non–red route				✓									✓							
Highway																					
Transport management	Red route		✓																✓	✓	✓
	Non–red route																				
Highways maintenance and works	Red route																				
	Non–red route		✓														✓	✓	✓		
Traffic signals	Red route		✓																✓		
	Non–red route																				
Street furniture	Red route		✓																✓		
	Non–red route			✓												✓		✓	✓	✓	
Utilities	Red route																				
	Non–red route															✓		✓	✓		
Abandoned cars	Red route		✓																✓		
	Non–red route																				
Landscaping	Red route			✓															✓		
	Non–red route																				
Skip licensing	Red route		✓																		
	Non–red route																				
Waste/litter	Red route		✓																		
	Non–red route			✓													✓				
Building																					
Maintenance and appearance	Red route				✓		✓				✓	✓	✓								
	Non–red route																				
Building control	Red route					✓															
	Non–red route																				
Footway																					
Obstructions	Red route		✓																✓		
	Non–red route																				
Maintenance private forecourts	Red route		✓								✓								✓		
	Non–red route																				
Street trading	Red route		✓	✓															✓		
	Non–red route																				
Public conveniences	Red route			✓																	
	Non–red route																				
Carriageway																					
Traffic management	Red route		✓						✓										✓		
	Non–red route																				
Parking	Red route		✓												✓		✓		✓		
	Non–red route																✓				
Buses	Red route		✓														✓			✓	
	Non–red route																				

Source: 10 interviews with agency staff with responsibilities in the Tooting area.

Table 6.3: Agency responsibilities for aspects of streets in London Road

	Sheffield City Council													Other										
	NCCD*		Development, Environment and Leisure Directorate									NCCD*												
			Environmental and Regulatory Services					Development Services																
Street	Sharrow Partnership Priority Area	Broomhill, Central and Nether Edge Panel	Environmental Services	Environmental Protection Services	Trading Standards	Waste Management	Health Protection Service	Planning Service	City Development Division	Transport and Highway Services	Street Force	Community Safety Team	Housing	South Yorkshire Police	TSC**	South Yorkshire Fire and Rescue Service	Business/home owner	Tenant/landlord/freeholder	Sheffield Homes	Royal Mail	South Yorkshire Passenger Transport Executive	Veolia Environmental Services	Bus operators	Utility companies
Economic development of town centre		✓																						
Environmental issues	✓		✓	✓																				
Planning								✓	✓															
Crime												✓		✓										
Advertising								✓																
Graffiti removal											✓													
Issuing and enforcing trading licences					✓		✓									✓								
Highway																								
Highways management										✓														
Highways maintenance and works										✓	✓													
Enforcement of highways regulations										✓	✓													
Traffic signals										✓	✓				✓									
Street furniture										✓	✓									✓	✓			✓
Utilities																				✓				✓
Abandoned cars											✓													
Landscaping											✓													
Waste/litter			✓			✓					✓						✓							
Building																								
Maintenance and appearance								✓									✓							
Building control								✓																
Footway																								
Obstructions										✓														
Maintenance of private forecourts																	✓							
Carriageway																								
Traffic management										✓	✓													
Parking										✓	✓													
Buses																					✓		✓	

*Neighbourhoods and Community Care Directorate. **Traffic Signals Centre.

Source: 10 interviews with agency staff with responsibilities in the London Road area.

owners of the building and the land. Finding out who owns a piece of land or a building, in order to facilitate redevelopment or to enforce proper maintenance, was mentioned by several agencies as a problem, leading to calls for more transparency of ownership.

Suitability of planning regulations

There were concerns and acknowledged dilemmas about how detailed and strict planning regulations on mixed-use high streets should be, and how much they are actually adhered to. Although planning regulations can require that a certain proportion of buildings should be type A1 retail, this does not specify the kinds of retail provision that are required, so they cannot prevent a centre being overrun by a particular type of business (for example, mobile phone shops). On the other hand, in some locations, planners face a dilemma between allowing the opening of a unit for a non-complying use, or keeping the building empty.

In addition, the local authority cannot influence what displays businesses put on their forecourts. This can be a particular problem, both visually and because goods displayed on forecourts significantly reduce the size of the footway and consequently how easily pedestrians can move through the area.

Appearance

The state of the buildings along a mixed-use street has a major impact on the image of the centre and how people feel about the area. While the local authority has the power to enforce maintenance standards on private buildings, forecourts and gardens if something is deemed to be unsafe, there is nothing it can legally do when something simply looks unsightly or neglected. For example, in Tooting, there are two businesses operating behind boarded-up windows.

Parked cars

It was reported that maintenance teams sometimes have difficulties in accessing areas because parked cars block their way. There is currently very limited legislation that allows councils to remove cars that are not parked illegally, making the maintenance teams reliant on the goodwill and availability of motorists to move their vehicles.

Street improvements

Under current arrangements, street improvements often have to be made piecemeal, by different agencies. In the case of street furniture, new signs are rarely integrated with existing street furniture and are often just added to what is already on the street. There are regulatory limits as to what extent this can be controlled.

Where funds had been allocated for environmental improvements, design project teams were criticised for not taking into account the views of all the professional groups and individuals affected by the scheme. A classic example cited was the failure to consult with the departments that have responsibility for maintaining the area. In such cases, the authority struggled to access certain items of street furniture, or found that the materials used were impractical for the job, difficult to clean, or cost too much to replace:

'It doesn't matter what you put in, how pretty it looks, if it's not possible to maintain it adequately it's soon going to be a waste of time.' (Service manager for public lighting and signage)

Related to this issue is the common lack of a standard pallet of materials for an area that design project teams can draw on when proposing new schemes. Consequently, each local authority may have a large variety of different types of street furniture and surfacing materials. This can both be unsightly and detract from a sense of common identity; it also means that maintenance teams have to stock a wide variety of replacement parts and invest more time in training staff to use different components and materials.

Issues associated with privatisation of services

Several concerns were raised about the impact of privatisation on the proliferation of waste on the street, the poor reinstatement of utility works, and the lack of local knowledge available to some private contractors and consultants.

Privatisation of commercial waste collection

Businesses are generally required by the local authority to arrange their own rubbish collection contracts. While the privatisation of commercial waste collection has increased competition, on some mixed-use streets it has had a marked negative effect on the street environment. Often several waste contractors now work in the same area collecting waste on different days, or at different times of the day. This can result in there always appearing to be refuse out on the street waiting to be collected.

As well as looking unsightly, and possibly smelling in the summer (depending on the type of rubbish), the presence of rubbish bags narrows the footway and the multiple vehicles visiting the area to collect waste contribute to congestion. Because there are multiple collection times, this also means that councils cannot send street cleaners into the area at a set time to comprehensively clean up after street collections.

The issue of waste being left on the street was mentioned as a problem in both Tooting and London Road; however, it was not felt to be an issue in Ball Hill, where the council undertakes the majority of commercial waste collection itself.

Privatisation of maintenance services

The subcontracting of day-to-day maintenance work to the private sector from the highway authority is increasingly common. In one area where this had occurred, there were concerns that the new consultancy staff lacked local knowledge and contacts, which made it much more difficult to operate efficiently, in close cooperation with people from other relevant agencies in the area.

Utilities

Utility companies do not pay any rent for occupying the area of street under which they place their cables and pipes, but the local authority often incurs considerable expense if it needs to move anything to undertake major street works. Officers felt that this relationship was unbalanced, and it was suggested that local authorities should charge utility companies a rent for placing their cables and pipes in the road, in order to offset some of these costs.

There was also criticism that utilities often do not have accurate records of where their services are located beneath the highway – which can be a significant cause of cost increases once street works are being carried out on site. In addition, when utility companies undertake their own works, they often fail to reinstate the footway or carriageway on a like-for-like basis, which puts an additional burden on councils to inspect works and then press for rectification of the deficiencies. All this detracts from the appearance of the street environment.

Organisational and management issues

A key feature of the smooth running of a town centre or a high street is good communication between all the agencies and individuals that have a part to play in planning, operating and maintaining the street. Members of the public are generally unaware of all the different organisations that run services in the area, and so do not know who to contact about particular problems. Several examples were given of departments and agencies that did not liaise with each other about the work they were planning to undertake in the same area. This could result in various problems such as conflicts of works, or teams undertaking unnecessary maintenance. The benefits to be gained from closer partnership working were widely recognised.

Boundaries of departmental responsibilities

The separation of responsibility between departments within a council can lead to inefficient working practices. For example, in one case study area the maintenance team has to maintain redundant signs, because it is not within its remit or budget to remove them; while in another area the separation of waste collection and street cleaning means that the two departments often have disputes about whose responsibility it is to remove a piece of waste.

Consistency of approach between adjoining areas

When different organisations have responsibility for managing adjoining areas, problems of consistency can arise, causing public concern or media ridicule. On the simplest level, an example was cited of one agency mowing a piece of land eight times a year, but the adjoining piece of land, managed by another organisation, only being mowed three or four times a year.

On a larger scale, adjacent approaches to street maintenance and management can be very different. This is perceived to be the situation in Tooting, where Wandsworth Borough Council manages Mitcham Road and TfL manages Upper Tooting Road. The feeling was expressed by several respondents that TfL did not provide the same level of service as the local council, because it was not locally based, both in terms of speed of action and understanding of local issues. More specifically:

- Because the highway ownership is divided, the council is restricted as to what it can do to improve the carriageway and footway in Tooting, as a part of improving the overall street environment in the town centre.

- There is a lot of street clutter, mainly centred on the Broadway junction where the two agencies' responsibilities overlap. This means that it is difficult to remove unwanted items, as both parties have to be consulted. As a result, it takes a long time to remove things and conditions can deteriorate in the meantime.
- Some officers in Wandsworth expressed a concern that the extra effort of trying to implement change in the Tooting area, compared with other town centres in the borough where they have full control, means that Tooting is in danger of receiving less priority than might otherwise be the case.

Partnership working

The local police were great exponents of the benefits of partnership working, partly through experience gained in the recently created Crime and Disorder Partnerships, and partly through an increased focus in some areas on community policing. Such partnerships usually involve a variety of local agencies such as the council, the health authority and the voluntary sector, to look at ways of solving local problems. Since all these agencies experience the problems of crime, there are major benefits in working together to pool resources and find inter-agency solutions. One area where there was felt to be room for improvement was the sharing of information, on an ongoing basis, between staff from different agencies represented on the street each day.

Tensions within local communities

The tensions between the twin primary functions of the street as a link and a place, and the different requirements of the various stakeholder groups using the street, can cause difficulties when conditions are reviewed and proposals put forward for changing the balance of street uses. Businesses can feel wary of the local authority's intentions and professional and cultural language problems can cause an extra layer of difficulty.

In Ball Hill, various tensions were exposed when the process of consultation was initiated, though they were later resolved. The city council called a consultation meeting with local businesses to consider how to improve bus reliability and air quality in Ball Hill, through improved traffic management and control measures. Although well advertised, this meeting was poorly attended. During the meeting, council officials put forward a suggested traffic scheme for discussion. Those attending misinterpreted the council's intentions and started a 'Ball Hill to close?' campaign, with petitions and posters in their shop windows. A second consultation meeting was hastily called, which was well attended, and the council was able to explain its aims and objectives more clearly. However, there were still concerns about the council's intentions and so a design workshop was set up, run in conjunction with the research team.

Design workshop in Ball Hill

At this workshop, which was attended by many local small businesses, the participants were split into design groups. Using large-scale maps of the high street area and acetate strips representing possible different street uses and street features, different solutions were sought to address the requirements of loading, parking, the various footway activities and the positioning of street furniture, and the location of bus stops. The ideas put forward have now been refined and are being implemented by the council and other agencies.

In Tooting and London Road, some tensions were apparent between different local population groups, often reflecting differences in attitudes and behaviour between the 'established' and 'incoming' populations. In Sheffield, for example, concerns were expressed among the incumbent population about a recent large influx of students resulting from the construction of a student housing complex at the northern end of London Road. Students were seen as a transitory group that was felt to contribute little to local economic and social life (only just over one third of students reported using London Road businesses on a regular basis), but was felt to put an extra strain on the local environment (for example, through adding to the amount of footway litter).

Summary

The intense and varied nature of the activities found on mixed-use streets inevitably produces a wide range of tensions and conflicts, both between and among the various link and place functions. These are currently recognised and managed with varying degrees of success, but they will need to be more explicitly identified and addressed if mixed-use streets are to realise their full potential as an attractive component of future sustainable urban communities.

These conflicts are to be found on the footway, at the kerbside and on the main carriageway. Some are better recognised than others, but they have not previously been so comprehensively documented in one report. Aspects that have received relatively little attention in the past include the dynamics of pedestrian and street furniture interactions on the footway, and the problems associated with high volumes of buses and bus passenger interchange – including the delays to traffic flow around busy bus stops, and the apparent presence of accident clusters around bus interchange stops.

This chapter has also documented the wide range of agencies with direct involvement in some aspect of the planning, design, management, operation and enforcement of street infrastructure and activity. Many of these agencies' activities are currently poorly coordinated, mainly due to lack of regulatory powers. In addition, the privatisation of many street functions and activities has resulted in a new set of problems and challenges.

In relation to wider stakeholder engagement, the message that emerges from this research is that taking account of the views of the different participants in the life of the street is important – but difficult. Such dissemination, consultation and empowerment activities need to be undertaken with care. There is a range of problems encountered by local authorities in trying to engage with local businesses, sometimes because they are part of larger entities and their local managers feel less involved. Other factors that may contribute to their lack of engagement with consultation processes include antipathy towards the local council and a general distrust of officialdom, language difficulties, or a feeling on the part of smaller businesses that they are too busy to get involved. It is clear that a carefully tailored approach to street-user consultation is needed.

7

Mixed-use local high streets: a key component of sustainable urban communities

Over the past few decades, traditional mixed-use urban high streets have largely been 'written off' by professionals, both as major centres for retail and commercial activity, and as an effective component of major urban transport routes and interchanges. Instead, the emphasis has been on providing purpose-built shopping centres, pedestrian-free traffic routes and off-road transport interchanges. However, this study has found that, far from being an outdated legacy of 19th-century English urban development, mixed-use local high streets are adapting to the consumer and citizen needs of the 21st century, despite a general lack of public sector investment, and have the potential to be key components of future urban sustainable communities. Their full potential is currently not being realised, for a variety of reasons.

This chapter first summarises the ways in which the case study mixed-use streets are already contributing positively to the government's sustainability and liveability agendas, despite their relative neglect, and argues the case for enhancing local high streets so that they can play a greater role in delivering part of the government's broader urban agenda. Next, we summarise the challenges that need to be addressed to overcome the problems and tensions experienced on the case study mixed-use streets, which, if not tackled, will prevent the realisation of their potential and may put at risk the future of the high street. We then consider ways in which some of these issues might be addressed, both in a general sense and with more specific recommendations for policy and practice. If these recommendations are adopted, we believe that mixed-use local high streets can play an important role in helping to retrofit existing urban areas to become more sustainable, and in contributing to the creation of new sustainable communities.

Sustainable urban communities: the current and potential contribution of mixed-use streets

This research has demonstrated that mixed-use local high streets already contribute in several ways to key government objectives for urban areas, both in relation to their link and place functions.

Encouraging more sustainable travel

The three case study streets are generally surrounded by large, highly permeable residential catchment areas that encourage residents to walk or cycle to retail, leisure and public facilities in their local area. However, for their economic survival, businesses also depend on customers drawn from further away. The evolution of these streets on arterial routes, served by high-frequency public transport services (bus and underground), means that they provide good accessibility for a wider base of regional customers, enabling many of them to use more sustainable means of transport than cars.

Supporting economically sustainable centres

Strong transport links, both regionally and locally, contribute to the economic sustainability of the local high street by providing good access for customers drawn from a wide catchment area. By providing vibrant centres for local business activity, the case study streets also contribute more generally to sustaining their local economies. Well-balanced mixed-use local high streets are able to achieve high levels of satisfaction among their local and visitor populations in terms of the services they provide. Businesses, too, found that mixed-use streets were good places for them to trade. The study found that there was no simple correlation between centre size and meeting local needs, however. In general, both Ball Hill and Tooting (the smallest and largest centres, respectively) were perceived to be very successful at meeting a broad range of local needs. By contrast, London Road was not, as it had a high proportion of takeaway shops and restaurants, and only one fresh food grocer.

Facilitating social inclusion

In general, the three case study areas appear to be able to attract a wide range of population groups, in terms of age and ethnicity, that are both representative of the local area and are drawn from a wider catchment area. The streets are accessible to those without access to a car, as well as to car drivers. While residents with mobility difficulties seemed to be using the case study streets less than in proportion to their numbers, all sites found a higher percentage of this group among visitors than residents, suggesting that mixed-use streets are relatively attractive to mobility impaired groups, perhaps because of their easy access by bus and on foot.

Providing community focus and local identity

Mixed-use streets provide a natural focal point where local people can meet friends, both formally and informally, by appointment or by chance. They offer many opportunities for unplanned encounters, and enable people to expand their personal horizons by observing those from other cultures and with other perspectives, in a non-threatening environment. The research found that a significant proportion of residents of long standing were likely to 'bump into' someone that they knew in their local high street. As important meeting places for social activity, mixed-use streets help to sustain and build local community capacity and social capital, and can contribute to reducing feelings of isolation and depression. For many people, the local high street represents the physical and cultural heart of their community, providing a valued sense of local identity.

Offering safe environments

Those interviewed perceived themselves to be relatively safe on the mixed-use streets, with only around a quarter of street users in each area stating that they felt personal safety to be an issue. There were no major differences here between residents and visitors, although women were generally more concerned than men about their safety. The threats that were perceived were localised and specific; in Tooting, these related to gangs of youths hanging around the streets mainly at night, and in London Road to alcoholics and drug users who gathered in a public space in front of a chemist's shop during the day.

However, although mixed-use local high streets appear to function well in many ways, contributing to several of the sustainability criteria, they are not generally perceived to be pleasant public spaces in which to spend time, either by local residents or visitors. Their physical environment does not contribute to environmental sustainability or liveability, thereby detracting from their attractiveness and risking undermining their future use, and hence their ongoing contribution to economic and social sustainability.

With careful design and management, and both public and private sector investment, we believe that local high streets can encourage more sustainable travel, reduce travel distances and foster local economic and social sustainability, in an environment that improves liveability and local quality of life.

However, the study identified a number of problem areas that represent serious challenges that need to be recognised and addressed before this vision can be realised.

Challenges confronting mixed-use streets

The successes of the case study streets were achieved despite tensions and problems that affected both their link and place functions, and had a detrimental effect on the streets as liveable spaces. Eight such problems, in particular, are identified below.

Dominance of traffic in the street scene

In traditional mixed-use streets over the past 50 years, the design of the high street has given priority to the link traffic function over the place activity function. In all three of the case study areas, the most significant problems that street users and residents identified related to the volumes of road traffic on the high street, and associated concerns about traffic dominance, including air pollution and traffic noise. Businesses also recognised these problems, but to a lesser extent. While maintaining their arterial function is crucial to the continuing economic and social success of the high street, ways need to be found to reduce traffic dominance and intimidation.

Conflicts among footway (pavement) uses and users

The footway is in general the most intensively used – and least explored – part of the mixed-use street. It contains a wide range of structures and street furniture, which can restrict movement and contribute to congestion. Many different agencies are responsible for installing and maintaining this range of items, so there is no coordination of their siting, and often no clear procedure for removing them once they become redundant. Among the groups of pedestrians using footways, there is a wide range of activity that has not hitherto been fully appreciated or investigated. Chapter 4 identified 10 kinds of pedestrian place users, each with their own set of footway requirements, many of whose needs are not catered for in current design guidance.

Traffic accidents

Danger from traffic when crossing the road was reported to be a major concern for between one quarter and one third of street users in each of the three study areas, with similar levels of concern found among the local business respondents. Analysis of the accident statistics showed clusters of pedestrian accidents at major road junctions, as well as in the vicinity of bars and pubs, particularly in the Tooting area at night. What has not hitherto been noted in the literature is the clustering of pedestrian accidents around busy bus stops. This is part of a wider challenge of designing for informal public transport interchange on the high street.

Exclusion of some population groups

We have already noted the relatively low use of mixed-use streets by people in wheelchairs and with other physical disabilities, although the study revealed generally higher levels of use among visitors in this category. Similarly, while adults with pushchairs were observed on the mixed-use streets, their numbers did not fully reflect the number of young children in the resident population, and it is unclear whether parents felt some inhibition from using these streets. This requires further examination.

Competing pressures on businesses

There were tensions between planners wishing to maintain diversity and commercial pressures to increase the uniformity of the type of businesses and services on offer. Local planners and residents generally welcome diversity, but once a particular commercial use is well established, there may be commercial pressures to open more businesses of the same type. Beyond a certain point, there is a risk that the street starts to lose its broad appeal, and becomes more vulnerable to changing fashions. There were related tensions between stagnation and gentrification. Older residents who have lived in the area for a long time often prefer things to remain the same, and bemoan the loss of certain shops and services. By catering more for a younger, and wealthier clientele, there is a risk that such areas will become gentrified, in some cases forcing out established residents through higher housing rents or prices, and alienating older residents through reductions in businesses catering for their specific needs.

Poor street appearance and cleanliness

The visual appearance of the street is an important factor, contributing to the overall image, identity and ambience of the area. Visual continuity in the building facades and coordinated shop fronts help to create a sense of identity and of place, but local planning authorities have limited resources to produce and enforce design guidance, and can only do this for new applications. The cleanliness of the street is also important to street users, not only in terms of the removal of graffiti, litter and abandoned articles, but also with regard to refuse collection. Refuse bags left lying in the street can restrict footway movement and are unsightly and sometimes smelly. The privatisation of refuse services has resulted in a multitude of service providers, each with different collection regimes. This can result in refuse bags lying on the footway for much of the day.

Lack of public amenities

In the street-user surveys, the amenity that users were overwhelmingly least satisfied with across all three areas was the provision of public toilets. The inadequate availability of seating and places to rest was the second highest concern. While the study found that public benches might be well used and well liked by a broad range of people, in some circumstances they can attract antisocial behaviour. In Tooting, toilets and benches had been removed for this reason. However, our survey evidence demonstrates that such closure and removal of public facilities is contrary to residents' and visitors' wishes, and contradicts government's express determination to improve inclusive aspects of the public realm. To resolve this dilemma, more attention needs to be paid to the precise siting and maintenance of such facilities. In addition, around 60% of respondents to the on-street interviews in each area were dissatisfied with number of public spaces and amount of greenery on and around the high street.

Diversity of agency responsibility and complexity of management

This study has documented the wide variety of uses and users of mixed-use streets: within the frontages, on the footway and in the carriageway, as well as beneath the street. Consequently, aspects of street planning, design and management inevitably draw in a wide range of public and private sector organisations, each with their own statutory or commercial interest, and with no single conductor orchestrating this complex symphony of activity. Over time, new street uses and organisations have arisen and others have vanished (particularly in the private sector), sometimes leaving behind a legacy of redundant items on the street. Invariably, this leads to an organisational situation that is complex and at times unclear, with potential gaps and overlaps. This all too often results in a street environment that is cluttered, dirty and has a neglected appearance – often in stark contrast to the tightly managed environment of the out-of-town shopping centre.

Solutions

It is gradually becoming apparent that – with careful planning, design and management – it is possible for mixed-use high streets to be both important and successful places *and* links in public and private transport networks, and to benefit from the interaction and vibrancy of both.

However, to be a secure part of the future and not just the past, mixed-use streets need to be better understood, better facilitated and better funded. Based on the various analyses from this study, and the views of the professionals and the public we consulted, the key ingredients for a successful mixed-use street would seem to include:

- a strong and diverse local and regional economic base;
- a socially well-balanced local community;
- good access to the high street, through a well-connected network of surrounding residential streets providing safe walking and cycling routes, high-quality, area-wide public transport networks and limited, short-stay parking provision;
- a broad range of local business and services, catering for a diversity of interests, and including public facilities such as libraries;
- a high-quality, clean and vibrant street environment, including well-designed footways, that provides a clear sense of local identity and includes important public spaces and amenities; and
- a commercial as well as a community sense of local ownership, and a responsiveness to changing social and market conditions.

The successful achievement of this vision will require a series of coordinated changes in approach, regulation and process, which can be grouped under four broad headings:

- adopt a balanced 'link and place' approach to mixed-use street planning and design;
- provide better coordination between agencies and street-user stakeholders;
- encourage enhanced information gathering and sharing; and
- provide more resources and powers.

Specific recommendations for policy and/or practice are highlighted beneath each discussion point, as appropriate.

Adopt a balanced 'link and place' approach to mixed-use street planning and design

There is an urgent need to end the conventional traffic-dominated approach to urban street planning and design. While mixed-use local high streets serve important transport link functions, both for private vehicles and public transport, their primary identity and role is provided through the place functions that they facilitate. A comprehensive and consistent approach to street planning and design is required that fully recognises and pays equal attention to the link and place functions of mixed-use streets. This will first require a better understanding and codification of the place functions of urban mixed-use streets.

In most high streets, this rebalancing is likely to require a shift in the current allocation of space provision, away from giving first priority to through traffic, to a greater concern with improving local access modes, and making better provision for footway activities, public amenities and public spaces. This rebalancing of priorities and space allocation is already starting to happen in some parts of the UK, such as Newland Avenue in Hull, Cowley Road in Oxford and Walworth Road in South London, with the twin objectives of improving the street environment and reducing accident rates.

One of the greatest design innovations will come from a recognition that footways cater for a wide range of pedestrian place activities – 10 have been identified in this study – and sensitively catering for them without formalising space use too much and so jeopardising the attractiveness that comes from the buzz of diverse, interacting and intensive street activity. Success is likely to depend on micro-aspects of design, such as the precise location and orientation of public seating, taking into account both their patterns of use and their impact on movement along the footway. Improvements also need to be skilfully introduced, so that they do not lead to commercial pressures that exclude the existing businesses or groups of people who have contributed to the character of the area.

Practice recommendations

The renaissance and re-engineering of the mixed-use high street, to meet the requirements of the 21st century, will require new approaches to street design and operation. This is likely to necessitate the introduction of a range of innovative and best-practice techniques, such as:

- reducing traffic dominance, accident risk and severance by widening footways, adding barrier-free median strips, planting greenery, providing extra controlled pedestrian crossings, and introducing 20mph zones;
- enabling street spaces to be used for different functions at different times of day, or day or the week (for example, using certain footway spaces for loading at night when streets are quieter, or allowing kerbside parking outside peak periods);
- improving provision for people in wheelchairs and those with pushchairs and buggies;

- providing street lighting that facilitates the various footway activities, assists with wayfinding and provides a strong sense of personal security, as well as meeting the needs of road traffic;
- reducing street clutter and improving the quality, attractiveness and cleanliness of the footway and frontages;
- improving and increasing the number of public amenities, such as seating, lighting and well-maintained public toilets, and providing a generally higher-quality public realm;
- developing design manuals to guide routine maintenance, shop-front improvements and new design interventions; and
- coordinating public transport provision to facilitate informal modal interchange and reduce traffic and pedestrian congestion, and accidents.

Policy recommendations

The recognition of the significance of mixed-use local high streets needs to occur at a strategic level in addition to the micro-scale, by:

- designating mixed-use local high streets as district centres in planning framework documents;
- recognising the place components of mixed-use local high streets in Local Transport Plans and Local Implementation Plans; and
- developing a comprehensive link/place approach to street planning and design.

Provide better coordination between agencies and street-user stakeholders

The case studies have highlighted the wide range of agencies that contribute to the functioning of the conventional mixed-use street. Their interests and priorities differ greatly, and few engage widely with other street-related professions, or have a direct interest in the ramifications of their actions on the street and street users as a whole. Even where there is an awareness of the broader context in which organisations operate, they often find it difficult to contact and engage meaningfully with other professional actors operating in the same area.

To overcome these problems, which lead to both inefficient resource use and a poorly integrated street environment, better coordination is needed among the numerous public and private sector agencies involved. The reported successes of the Crime and Disorder Partnerships hint at what might be achieved through closer coordination and partnership working – to a set of locally agreed, cross-sector objectives. The success of Tooting as a centre suggests that a post similar in concept to the town centre manager should be adopted to sustain and develop mixed-use streets. In smaller urban centres, this post could be combined with other roles within an authority or devolved to a street scene department.

The 2004 Traffic Management Act places a duty on the highway authority to ensure the efficient movement of all traffic (including pedestrians) and coordinate street works on, or in the vicinity of, main routes in order to minimise disturbances. This should encourage highway authorities to improve communications with and between the other key street players. However, some agencies appear to have interpreted this new duty rather narrowly, thereby reinforcing the link dominance on the high street. Central government should urgently clarify the need to take into account the place requirements on mixed-use streets. A good starting point would be to establish quality management processes for all maintenance issues and new schemes involving mixed-use streets, to which different departments and agencies could contribute and consult on.

A key message is that stakeholder engagement is a vital part of the process of creating sustainable mixed-use streets, and is an ongoing exercise. The Ball Hill case study showed that it takes considerable efforts to build up the trust of local communities and harness their knowledge and enthusiasm. Stakeholder engagement is now firmly established in policy and practice, and a diverse range of communication channels and techniques are required. One particular problem that has been highlighted by this study is that special efforts need to be made to ensure a constructive engagement with businesses. Large businesses may not have a management team with an interest in the local area, or authority to act, and small local traders may be unused to this type of partnership working with local authorities and other professional groups.

Practice recommendations

- Establish inter-departmental working within the local authority to manage the quality of mixed-use local high streets – precedents include setting up a town centre manager post for larger centres. Some local authorities are setting up street scene departments that provide cross-cutting services.
- Ensure that private companies, whether consultants or contractors, are fully aware of local objectives and practices.
- Establish a forum for all stakeholders in the street, to include the relevant local authority departments, the transport authority, local businesses and residents. Regeneration partnerships and town centre management groups provide a model.
- Encourage the development of more innovative forms of design workshop, along the lines outlined in Chapters 5 and 6, to actively engage a wide range of stakeholders in problem identification, future visioning and design.

Encourage enhanced information gathering and sharing

As this report has shown, a huge variety and volume of data are needed to contribute to an understanding of how mixed-use streets operate, to identify current shortcomings, and to plan meaningfully for more sustainable, liveable and socially inclusive streets.

The data required to achieve this are held by many agencies, in different formats, covering different time periods and spatial units, using different definitions and designed for different analysis packages. Thus, much effort will need to be put into data collection and collation, to better understand the asset base, the various street-user needs and the problems requiring action. This will require a greater willingness on the part of the agencies involved to share data, and to make them available in a compatible format. Utility agencies, waste collection companies and the police all need to be involved.

Once the data have been assembled, it will be possible to measure the performance of the street, along a number of link and place dimensions. Agreement will be required among the various agencies on how to measure street performance and how to benchmark this against comparable streets, in order to identify areas where priority attention should be paid and to agree targets for improvement.

Businesses also need more information about their customers; how they access their services and the concerns that they have about the street. The community street audit mechanism is a relatively simple way for local stakeholders to gather and record meaningful data about their street. Stakeholder consultation is important, but needs to take place in a context where all parties have full access to information about each party's intentions and objectives.

Practice recommendations

- Develop a GIS-based system for collating and analysing these diverse and complex data sets, with one agency tasked with this function.
- Set up agreements with the various street agencies for ongoing data sharing and supply to the designated agency.
- Agree a set of street performance indicators and targets for street improvement.
- Use community street audits, which provide a comparatively straightforward and low-cost method for establishing issues and potential improvements.

Provide more resources and powers

Local authorities already have a number of powers to address many of the challenges raised in this report. Problems arise both with communication and collaboration between departments and agencies, and because local authorities do not have the resources effectively to use the powers they do possess. For example, businesses have a legal Duty of Care under the 1990 Environmental Protection Act to put out waste for collection on or near the collection time, and for no longer than necessary. However, to educate businesses or to enforce the Act requires resources. Carrying out the recommendations set out above will involve the provision of some extra staff and associated financial resources.

The study has also identified circumstances in which local authorities have the will but lack the means to take action. An example of this is ensuring that shop owners maintain their premises to a reasonable standard. In these instances, further investigation needs to be undertaken into whether extra regulatory powers are feasible or desirable.

Finally, some of the apparent neglect of the condition of the high street is due to a lack of significant investment in the physical infrastructure of the street, apart from the road surface and particular items of private sector street furniture, over several decades. Providing a high-quality public realm, together with high-quality public amenities, will require substantial investment and ongoing maintenance costs. Some larger urban centres are funding some of this work in conjunction with Business Improvement Districts, but simpler financial models will be needed for most traditional high streets. Here more work is needed to establish clear economic, social and environmental business cases for such investments.

Policy recommendations

- Provide more resources or divert existing resources to local authority departments with a responsibility for mixed-use local high streets. Resources should be for day-to-day enforcement, cleanliness and ongoing maintenance, as well as for new schemes that improve street quality and the range of public amenities.
- Develop a business case framework for substantial investment in mixed-use high streets, as a cornerstone of the delivery mechanisms for future sustainable communities, and explore new funding mechanisms, including locally generated sources.
- Investigate the potential for new regulatory powers to require:
  - shop and other business owners to maintain their fronts to a reasonable standard;
  - all agencies that install street furniture and infrastructure to agree the precise location, shape and construction of the structure with the local highway or planning authority; and
  - utility companies to keep adequate records of the location of their pipes and cables, and to reinstate the street surface using original materials.

Conclusion

This report set out to explore everyday life on mixed-use streets: how they are used on a daily basis and what those who contribute to their operation or visit them think about them. Although still largely viewed as relics of a bygone age by many professionals, and an impediment to the creation of the 20th-century vision of a modern city, we found a very different picture among those for whom they are an integral part of daily life.

Most people liked visiting their local high street, which contributed an important part of their local identity, provided a focal point for informal social contact, and in most cases contained a wide range of high-quality businesses that were highly valued. This general support for mixed-use streets arose despite very strong concerns about the poor quality of the outdoor street environment: the dominance of road traffic and the cluttered, ill-coordinated and unkempt nature of much of the public realm – in particular, the footway.

While such streets have been neglected by professionals in the past, looked at through fresh eyes they offer solutions to some of the problems that planners, engineers and designers face in designing more sustainable and inclusive urban forms for the future. They encourage sustainable travel and provide local identity and centres of social and economic activity. However, to realise this potential, changes are required in the ways in which high streets are planned, designed and managed – both in terms of conception and process – with an explicit recognition of the need to accommodate and balance various competing link and place functions in new, imaginative ways.

Resolving the problems posed by seeking to make mixed-use streets a cornerstone of future sustainable communities is no small challenge. Here the words of Donald Appleyard provide inspiration that is as relevant to mixed-use streets today as it was when he wrote it in 1982:

> The economist sees the resolution of these different demands in terms of compromise and trade-offs, but the urban designer and planner can offer creative ingenuity and the ability to serve several group needs within a limited space. By designing the street to be used to capacity, each group can be attracted to its particular amenities; new functions and meanings can be imagined that will return the street to the center of public life and make it once more the arena for supporting the culture of cities. (Cited in Moudon, 1991, p 8)

There has been a gap of over one hundred years between the development of the traditional high street and efforts to incorporate similar principles in some of the new master plans for sustainable communities, where the value of this form of street is again beginning to be recognised.

Within existing built-up areas, the mixed-use high street is well placed to have a bright future. But it will require imagination, determination and substantial funding to fully realise its potential, and bring it up to the standard required of a 21st-century high street. If this is done, the local high street can provide the cornerstone of efforts needed to retrofit the many existing urban areas to become future sustainable communities.

References

Allen, C., Camina, M., Casey, R., Coward, S. and Wood, M. (2005) *Mixed Tenure Twenty Years On: Nothing out of the Ordinary*, York: Chartered Institute of Housing/Joseph Rowntree Foundation.

Anderson, E. (2004) 'The cosmopolitan canopy', *Annals of the American Academy of Political and Social Science*, no 595, pp 14-31.

Appleyard, D. (1981) *Liveable Streets*, Berkeley, CA: University of California Press.

Armitage, R. (2002) *To CCTV or not to CCTV? A Review of Current Research into the Effectiveness of CCTV Systems in Reducing Crime*, London: Nacro.

Atkinson, R. (2003) 'Domestication by cappuccino or a revenge on urban space? Control and empowerment in the management of public spaces', *Urban Studies*, vol 40, no 9, pp 1829-43.

Barton, H., Grant, M. and Guise, R. (2003) *Shaping Neighbourhoods: A Guide for Health, Sustainability and Vitality*, London: Spon Press.

Batty, M. (1997) 'The retail revolution', *Environment and Planning B*, 29, pp 1-2.

Baxter, A. and Associates in association with EDAW (2002) *Paving the Way: How we Achieve Clean, Safe and Attractive Streets*, Tonbridge: Thomas Telford for the Commission for Architecture and the Built Environment and the Office of the Deputy Prime Minister.

Berube, A. (2005) *Mixed Communities in England: A US Perspective on Evidence and Policy Prospects*, York: Joseph Rowntree Foundation.

Bianchini, F. (1995) 'Night cultures, night economies', *Planning Practice and Research*, vol 10, no 2, pp 121-6.

Bromley, R., Tallon, A. and Thomas, C. (2003) 'Disaggregating the space-time layers of city centre activities and their users', *Environment and Planning A*, vol 35, pp 1831-51.

Buchanan, C.D. (1963) *Traffic in Towns: A Study of the Long-Term Problems of Traffic in Urban Areas*, London: HMSO.

CABE (Commission for Architecture and the Built Environment)/MORI (2002) *Streets of Shame: Executive Summary*, London: CABE/MORI.

CABE (2004) *Design Reviewed Town Centre Retail: Lessons Learnt from Projects Reviewed by CABE's Expert Design Panel*, London: CABE.

Carmona, M., de Magalhäes, C., Hammond, L., Blum, R. and Yang, D. with Buro Happold (2004) *Living Places: Caring for Quality*, London: The Stationery Office.

Commission for Integrated Transport (2006) *Sustainable Transport Choices and the Retail Sector*, Auth. Mott MacDonald (www.cfit.gov.uk/docs/2006/stc/index.htm).

Coupland A. (ed) (1997) *Reclaiming the City: Mixed-use Development*, London: E & FN Spon.

Cullen, G. (1971) *The Concise Townscape*, Oxford: Architectural Press.

Davis, C. (1996) 'Streetscape' (www.buildingconservation.com/articles/scape/scape.htm).

Desyllas, J. (2006) 'The cost of bad street design', in Commission for Architecture and the Built Environment, *The Cost of Bad Design*, London: Commission for Architecture and the Built Environment.

DETR (Department for Environment, Transport and the Regions) (1998) *Places, Streets and Movement: A Companion Guide to Design Bulletin 32 Residential Roads and Footpaths*, London: DETR.

DETR (1999) *Towards an Urban Renaissance: Final Report of the Urban Task Force Chaired by Lord Rogers of Riverside*, London: DETR.

DETR and CABE (Commission for Architecture and the Built Environment) (2000) *By Design – Urban Design in the Planning System: Towards Better Practice*, London: Thomas Telford.

DTLR (Department for Transport, Local Government and the Regions) (2002) *Green Spaces, Better Places: Final Report of the Urban Green Spaces Task Force*, London: DTLR.

De Vasconcellos, A. (2004) 'The use of streets: A reassessment and tribute to Donald Appleyard', *Journal of Urban Design*, vol 9, no 1, pp 3-22.

DoE (Department of the Environment) (1995) *Quality in Town and Country: Urban Design Campaign*, London: DoE.

DoE (1996) *Planning Policy Guidance Note 6: Town Centres*, London: Her Majesty's Stationery Office.

Duany, A. (2003) 'Neighbourhood design in practice', in P. Neal (ed) *Urban Villages and the Making of Communities*, London: Spon Press.

Eames, M. and Adebowale, M. (eds) (2002). *Sustainable Development and Social Inclusion: Towards an Integrated Approach to Research*, York: Joseph Rowntree Foundation/YPS.

English Heritage (2000) *Streets for All: A Guide to the Management of London's Streets*, London: English Heritage.

Engwitcht, D. (2005) *Mental Speed Bumps: The Smarter Way to Tame Traffic*, Annandale, Australia: Envirobooks.

Gans, H. (1968) *People and Plans: Essays on Urban Problems and Solutions*, New York, NY and London: Basic Books.

Gehl, J. (1996) *Life Between Buildings: Using Public Space* (3rd edn), Skive, Copenhagen: Arkitektens Forlag.

Gehl Architects (2004) *Towards a Fine City for People: Public Spaces and Public Life – London*, London: Central London Partnership and Transport for London.

Hamilton-Baillie, B. and Jones, P. (2005) 'Improving traffic behaviour and safety through urban design', Paper 14014, *Proceedings of the Institution of Civil Engineering*, 158, pp 39-47.

Hass-Klau, C. (1999) *Streets as Living Space: Helping Public Places Play their Proper Role*, London: Landor Publishing.

Hebbert, M. (1998) *London: More by Fortune than Design*, Chichester: John Wiley & Sons.

Hebbert, M. (2005) 'Engineering, urbanism and the struggle for street design', *Journal of Urban Design*, vol 10, no 1, pp 39-60.

Highways Agency (1994) *Design Manual for Roads and Bridges*, London: HMSO.

Hillier, B. (1996) 'Cities as movement economies', *Urban Design International*, vol 1, no 1, pp 47-60.

Hillier, B. (2004) 'Can streets be made safe?', *Urban Design International*, vol 9, no 1, pp 31-45.

Hollands, R. and Chatterton, P. (2003) 'Producing nightlife in the new urban entertainment economy: corporatization, branding and market segmentation', *International Journal of Urban and Regional Research*, vol 27, no 2, pp 361-85.

Home Office and Office of the Deputy Prime Minister (2003) *Safer Places: The Planning System and Crime Prevention*, London: Home Office.

ICE (Institution of Civil Engineers) (2002) *The 2002 Design Streets for People Report*, Tonbridge: Thomas Telford.

Ishaque, M.M. (2006) 'Policies for pedestrian access: multi-modal trade-off analysis using micro simulation techniques', Unpublished PhD Thesis, Imperial College, London.

Jacobs, J. (1961) *The Death and Life of Great American Cities: The Failure of Town Planning*, Harmondsworth: Penguin Books in association with Jonathan Cape.

Jones, P., Marshall, S. and Boujenko, N. (2007) *Link and Place: A Guide to Street Planning and Design*, London: Landor Publishing.

Lucas, K., Walker, G., Eames, M., Fay, H. and Poustie, M. (2004) *Environment and Social Justice: Rapid Research and Evidence Review*, London: Policy Studies Institute.

Mintel (2004) *High Streets Pubs and Bars: UK April 2004*, London: Mintel International Group Ltd.

Moudon, A.V. (ed) (1991) *Public Streets for Public Use*, New York, NY: Columbia University Press.

ODPM (Office of the Deputy Prime Minister) (2002) *Living Places – Cleaner, Safer, Greener*, London: The Stationery Office.

ODPM (2005) *Planning Policy Statement 1: Delivering Sustainable Development*, London: The Stationery Office.

ODPM (Office of the Deputy Prime Minister) (2006) *Planning Policy Statement 6: Planning for Town Centres*, London: The Stationery Office.

OECD (Organisation for Economic Cooperation and Development) (1974) *Streets for People*, Paris: OECD.

Page, B., Duffy, B. and Atkinson, S. (2002) *The Rising Prominence of Liveability*, London: MORI.

Pain, R. (2001) 'Gender, race, age and fear in the city', *Urban Studies*, vol 38, no 5-6, pp 899-913.

Raco, M. (2003) 'Remaking place and securitising space: urban regeneration and the strategies, tactics and practices of policing in the UK', *Urban Studies*, vol 40, no 9, pp 1869-87.

Roberts, M. (2004) *Good Practice in Managing the Evening and Night-time Economies: A Literature Review from an Environmental Perspective*, London: ODPM.

SEU (Social Exclusion Unit) (2003) *Making Connections: Final Report on Transport and Social Exclusion*, London: SEU and ODPM.

Shared Space (2005) 'Room for everyone: a new vision for public spaces', (www.shared-space.org).

Tibbalds, F. (1992) *Making People Friendly Towns: Improving the Public Environment in Towns and Cities*, Harlow: Longman.

Trancik, R. (1986) *Finding Lost Space: Theories of Urban Design*, New York, NY: Van Nostrand Reinhold.

URBED (Urban and Economic Development Group) (1994) *Vital and Viable Town Centres: Meeting the Challenge*, London: HMSO.

Whyte, W.H. (1980, reprinted 2001) *The Social Life of Small Urban Spaces*, New York, NY: Project for Public Places.

Whyte, W.H. (1988) *City: Rediscovering the Centre*, New York, NY: Doubleday.

Wrigley, N., Guy, C. and Lowe, M. (2002) 'Urban regeneration, social inclusion and large store development: the Seacroft development in context', *Urban Studies*, vol 39, no 11, pp 2101-14.

Zukin, S. (1995) *The Culture of Cities*, Cambridge, MA: Blackwell.